The Design of Herman Miller

John M Haynes
Presented to me by
Pat Conway
April 1978

The Design of Herman Miller
By Ralph Caplan

WHITNEY LIBRARY OF DESIGN, an imprint of
WATSON-GUPTILL PUBLICATIONS, New York, N.Y.

All photographs and drawings in this book were made available through the courtesy of Herman Miller.

Copyright © 1976 by Ralph Caplan
First published 1976 in New York by Whitney Library of Design,
an imprint of Watson-Guptill Publications,
a division of Billboard Publications, Inc.,
1515 Broadway, New York, N.Y. 10036

All rights reserved. No part of this publication
may be reproduced or used in any form or by any means—graphic,
electronic, or mechanical, including photocopying, recording, taping,
or information storage and retrieval systems—without
written permission of the publisher.

Manufactured in U.S.A.

Library of Congress Cataloging in Publication Data
Caplan, Ralph.
  The design of Herman Miller.
  1. Miller (Herman) Furniture Company, Inc., Zeeland,
Mich. 2. Furniture design. I. Title.
TS880.C36 1976   338.7′61′749217415   76-6489
ISBN 0-8230-7141-3

First Printing, 1976

Edited by Susan Braybrooke and Susan Davis
Designed by Michel Goldberg
Set in 11 point Helvetica by Gerard Associates/Graphic Arts, Inc.

Contents

Foreword by Benjamin Thompson	6
Preface	9
The View from Madison Avenue	10
Zeeland: The Soil	14
D. J. De Pree: The Roots	16
Early Growth: Rohde	24
The Flowering of Design: Nelson, Eames, Girard	30
Branching Out: Propst	73
My Life in an Action Office	84
Redesigning the Family Tree	92
New Limbs	102
Shoptalk	110
Baptism and Chicken Soup	112
What Day Is It?: Frost	114
Collision Insurance	118

Foreword

This fascinating book tells an intimate adventure story about the world of design. It is fascinating to me because it is crammed with songs my childhood never taught me, things I never knew although I had thought of Herman Miller as familiar territory. What makes it important is that, in my view, the act of doing anything for the first time is impossible. At Herman Miller, though, they succeeded because they found a special equation for doing. More important, they found a cast of characters able to act out that special equation.

That much I knew. Back in 1952, when a small clutch of architects was struggling to get commissions for modern buildings (and most of them were lucky to be building small houses, mainly for themselves), I opened a design store in a single room on Brattle Street in Cambridge, Massachusetts. I was one of those struggling architects, painfully aware from our early years of practice that, once the glorious shell was completed, there was virtually nothing compatible that the pioneering owner or designer could conveniently buy to sit or eat on. Assembling the ingredients of the interior environment became the mission of our shop, which we named Design Research. We traveled widely here and abroad to find furnishings for every conceivable human need. One of the rare and valuable American sources of furniture in those days was Herman Miller of Zeeland, Michigan. Yet, aside from the address, little was known about Miller—that's the stuff of this story.

Until I read *The Design of Herman Miller,* I had never heard of D. J. De Pree. I thought Miller of Michigan was the man behind the wheel. I had no idea how much the design world owed to this inexperienced small-town businessman whose religious principles led him to stumble on a secret for becoming an effective client: this man actually listened, even to designers.

One of the designers De Pree listened to was George Nelson. We *had* heard of Nelson, through his writing in professional journals and his efforts with Storagewall. Organized storage had become a functional requirement in most contemporary interiors, but the idea that you could commercially buy an entire wall of it was new and important. Its announcement was a great step forward.

Another such moment came when Miller's first plywood "potato chip" chairs appeared in their neat cardboard boxes. Contemporary furniture at that time was usually shipped in heavy wooden crates and arrived broken. Wrestling with the Railway Express and insurance companies was the most painful chore in furniture retailing. You sometimes had to order two or three backup chairs in order to receive one intact. Suddenly here was Herman Miller with a technological chair discovery that was not only comfortable to sit on, but conveniently packaged in a cardboard box that solved the shipping problem. Everyone who came to the store studied the welded rubber connections and the molded plywood, asking "Who is Charles Eames?" I studied the shipping box. I was asking, "Who is Herman Miller, anyway?" What kind of place is Zeeland, Michigan, which can solve two problems at once?

Caplan's book unwinds the secrets: Zeeland was a place subject to all the pressures that had made "Grand Rapids" a pejorative design term. But it was also a place that had a labor pool responsive to D. J. De Pree's obsession with quality, even though the quality took the form of products that may have looked funnier in Zeeland than in Cambridge.

Geography is as important to the Herman Miller story as it is to a Western movie. I didn't expect that, although I might have. The Midwest is a special kind of place, and I can speak for it, since I came from across Lake Michigan in Minnesota. There is luck to the story told, and maybe Herman Miller was just lucky to have been born around Zeeland. But the complete cast of characters mentioned is not Midwestern. George Nelson must have taken the Michigan Central sleeper out of Grand Central — a New Yorker who would disgorge his sophisticated insights on De Pree's Midwest doorstep. Not long after — and at Nelson's urging — came the free-thinking California designer and filmmaker, Charles Eames. Soon after came Sandro Girard, architect and colorist from Santa Fe, New Mexico. Then from Colorado arrived inventor Robert Propst. What a curious gang of outsiders to face at an 8 A.M. Midwest business meeting!

Eames' chairs soon became Herman Miller's most famous design product. Nelson designed a wider range of desks, sofas, bureaus, and storage pieces, but the Herman Miller Company was not marketing furniture for retail sales and the price structure did not work for D/R. Yet for many years we displayed the chairs particularly. We couldn't stand not having them around, just so our design customers would know what a friend really ought to be like.

Ralph Caplan has written this as an adventure story, I guess on the premise that the truth is good enough. It is. Chronicles of creative experiences after the fact are mostly romanticized bunk. The story of Van Gogh's moods and the trials of Michelangelo generally come across like lathery soap operas. In the business world, *Fortune* magazine features a monthly saga of some corporate man's success. But do we ever follow the false starts and failures that describe the human creative journey? Sometimes we do. But until now I hadn't read one about the design world.

It's been my experience that high peaks of creativity within groups last about ten years. That was true of the Bauhaus and other comparable adventures. Yet Herman Miller continued its period of creativity long after that initial ten years were up. This is remarkable in view of the fact that the creative act is a bore to beholders. No thinking corporation will permit it for long; no serious institution can stomach indescribable confusion. Creativity is too challenging to the permanent staff and too wasteful in the eyes of bankers and controllers. Its odd pattern is dislocating to any well-adjusted person's normal day. Maybe the man who can tolerate the continuing atmosphere of creativity is the most creative of all. Such a man was D. J. De Pree.

Apparently he did more than tolerate creativity. He ignited the stuff by latching onto first-class people and giving them their design head. These special individuals were all ahead of the design mainstream and they listened to the wind. Thus Miller and friends enriched the design world.

Caplan, in revealing how it happened, treats the company as if it were a man, and shows us that under optimum circumstances there are significant similarities between the two — enough to have produced a very special creative partnership.

Benjamin Thompson, FAIA
Cambridge, Massachusetts

Left to right: Robert Propst, Alexander Girard, George Nelson, D. J. De Pree, and Ray and Charles Eames, at the November 25, 1975, opening of the Walker Art Center's massive Herman Miller exhibition—the only time all five designers have ever been together. Photograph by Melissa Brown.

Preface

This book represents a small triumph of discovery over prejudice — my own prejudice. Although I was determined at the outset to avoid such staples as company history and a biography of the founder, I did not succeed and am glad I didn't. The history turned out to be fascinating, and the fascination kept leading back to the founder, D. J. De Pree.

In the Foreword Benjamin Thompson asks the question: Who is Herman Miller anyway? Well, there is Herman Miller the corporation and there was Herman Miller the man. Herman Miller the man supplied the capital for Herman Miller the furniture company, managed by D. J. De Pree, who in the twenties also managed the Herman Miller Clock Company. There is today a Howard Miller Clock Company, but in those days Howard Miller — who is Herman Miller's son — worked at the Herman Miller Clock Company while Herman Miller was managing a clock company of another name.

Even in Zeeland it isn't an easy story to keep straight.

In researching the book I interviewed scores of designers and Herman Miller managers, employees, former employees, suppliers, customers, and competitors. That is, of course, standard procedure. But the writing procedure was not standard: in order to see the company's Action Office facilities in action, I installed myself in Herman Miller's New York headquarters. Strange as it seems, and was, the book was written in a showroom.

I accumulated a large pile of debts along the way. There are far too many creditors for a complete list, but some must be acknowledged: Bob Blaich, John Buglisi, D. J. De Pree, Hugh De Pree, Max De Pree, Charles Eames, Jimmy Eppinger, Steve Frykholm, Hilda Longinotti, Adelle Maronna, George Nelson, Larry Pond, Tom Pratt, Bob Propst, Judith Ramquist, Thelma Rawlings, Carl Ruff, and Herman Miller's entire New York staff, who tolerated my unexplained presence with a singular lack of suspicion. More suspicious, but indispensable, were my research assistants, Mary Cunniff and Ann Ludwig.

All of the above contributed hugely to this project. They are of course not responsible for my opinions or for any errors of fact.

Ralph Caplan

The Design of Herman Miller

The View from Madison Avenue

Herman Miller Inc., of Zeeland, Michigan, is in a state of transition. That gives it something in common with all other corporations in the Western world. To understand the company you have to see what it is in transition from and to. A good place to start is the company's showroom on Madison Avenue in New York City, for it is a palpable statement of where the company finds itself, has been, is headed.

Stepping off the elevator, you are at once confronted by a receptionist charged with finding out who you are and who sent you. That requested information is a hangover from the days when sales were made only through architects or designers, a selling mechanism traditional in the industry and pioneered by Herman Miller.

But when you look past the receptionist's head what you see is an area full of something not traditional in the furniture industry and not — strictly speaking — furniture. It looks like furniture, but is conceived and sold as something else. You face a network of open work spaces in a variety of configurations made from components of Action Office, a Herman Miller system of related products designed after long and painstaking research into office behavior. Some of these spaces have sales or showroom personnel in them. A few are empty and have been set up for demonstration purposes.

Action Office was conceived more than ten years ago by inventor Robert Propst, who had no specific interest in furniture as such — he has even less interest in it now — but was keenly interested in how work gets done in offices. Action Office is now Herman Miller's largest single product line.

One corner of the showroom is given to another Propst creation called Co/Struc (for "Coherent Structures"). This is a materials-management system of plastic containers, frames, carts and rails for hospitals and other health-care facilities. Like Action Office, Co/Struc is modular, movable, adjustable, and panel- or wall-hung. Its social purpose is to provide hospitals with facilities to help make them more effective and less costly. Its commercial purpose is to make Herman Miller a major supplier to the $250-million health-care market. Combined with Action Office and supportive Herman Miller seating, Co/Struc can form the basis for a complete hospital interior, as it does at the Central Medical Pavilion in Pittsburgh.

In the showroom's Co/Struc area there is a hospital room complete with everything but a patient. The bed is a standard hospital crank bed, covered with a multicolored spread designed, as are all Herman Miller fabrics, by Alexander Girard. The rest of the equipment, except for a couple of Eames chairs, is Co/Struc.

So much for systems. On the other side of the showroom is a collection of contemporary furniture, including some of the most presti-

Eames walnut stool.

gious pieces ever made. In sensuous contrast to the aggressively functional Action Office and Co/Struc parts, here are rosewood and walnut and rich leathers and fabrics.

Almost at dead center of the showroom there sits an Eames stool designed in 1960. If you sit on it and face east, you see Action Office components. If you face west, your eye takes in an expanse of elegant chairs by Charles Eames and Poul Kjaerholm.

To sit in the center of the showroom is to sit in the center of the Herman Miller situation. The corporate focus has shifted so radically that in a 1973 speech President Hugh De Pree found it necessary to remind the company that office and health-care business was not Herman Miller's *only* business. "Furniture forms the third and *equally* important part of a three-pronged effort," he said.

The products displayed on one side, then, represent a company that brings researchers, designers, health-care experts, and salespeople together to solve problems of institutional life and to sell the solutions at a profit. The products on the other side reveal a manufacturer of chairs, sofas, tables, credenzas, desks, and stools.

Which is the real Herman Miller? They both are, of course. But in another sense, the real Herman Miller can't be found at either end of the New York showroom. For that you have to go to

The Design of Herman Miller The View from Madison Avenue

The Design of Herman Miller The View from Madison Avenue

Juxtaposition of sensuous piece goods with plain work station systems in showroom dramatizes paradox in the design of Herman Miller.

The Design of Herman Miller   Zeeland: The Soil

Zeeland, Michigan, where founder D. J. De Pree was born, is today astonishingly like Zeeland, Michigan, *when* D. J. De Pree was born. During those 84 years time hasn't stood still exactly, but neither has it produced the kind of effect most American communities have experienced. There are still no bars, no pool halls, no theaters. There are 32 industries and 13 churches, with services held twice on Sunday.

Architect Quincy Jones has developed a master plan for new plant and executive facilities in Zeeland that are now being built. At this writing the company is housed in three buildings: the factory designed by George Nelson in 1962; Ad East, a former factory, now the administrative headquarters, where the president, chairman of the board, and treasurer have their offices; and Ad West, the operational headquarters, with offices for marketing, communications, sales, health sciences, word processing, and design. Between Ad East and Ad West sits another neighborhood industry — Big Dutchman, manufacturers of livestock-feeding equipment.

Ad West is a spectacularly undistinguished building, leased from Big Dutchman and recently converted to Action Office facilities. Behind it is the parking lot of the Top Line Hog Company, and from the north windows of Ad West you can see a fleet of Top Line trucks, with tailgates bearing the admonition: EAT MORE PORK.

Anyone inclined to obey can do so happily at Van Raalte's restaurant, where at lunchtime you are likely to encounter Herman Miller's son Howard. Or you can drive to adjacent Holland, a tulip-embroidered town upon which entrepreneurs have imposed a Dutch Disneyland of wooden shoes, windmills, and plaster-of-Paris flower gardens.

Zeeland has traditional small town problems. The young complain that there is nothing to do and no place to go, at least on nights when the churches are closed. It also has contemporary small-town problems. Theaterless it may be, but television brings bad tidings from the world beyond. Predictably, some crack under the strain; and one of the churches, finding psychiatry godless on the one hand and necessary on the other, has established its own treatment institution, called Pine Rest.

For the most part, though, Zeeland has the solidity and stolidity it appears to have. "George Nelson used to talk about 'the Zeeland peculiar,'" D. J. De Pree says. "But we have a climate here for quality. The people are dependable, cooperative, peaceful, and thrifty — and they are taught all that from the pulpit."

The Design of Herman Miller   Zeeland: The Soil

Zeeland city hall; barn in nearby Saugatuck; Main Street, Zeeland; Top Line Hog Company truck. Photographs by Gary Van Dis.

The Design of Herman Miller

D. J. De Pree: The Roots

The story of a company, like the story of a living man, contains certain basic components: the origins, the heritage, the present, and speculation toward the future. But to describe either man or company in these linear terms is at best boring and at worst deceptive. Even when prepared with the best of intentions and the most painstaking accuracy, company stories often turn out to be lies.

The reason may lie in what is left out. *Origin,* after all, is simply a matter of where it all started. *Heritage* is just an account of the baggage that has been hauled along on the trip. The present, once it has been encased in prose, is merely another kind of past. And even future speculation is likely to be experienced not as a leap, but as a laundry list of possible landings.

Those elements are static both in themselves and in combination. They spring to life only when animated by a sense of roots. The roots of a company are the dynamic process by which its present and future feed upon its past. Roots are alive and have to stay alive to do their job. (Blossoms can work for a while posthumously.)

The uniqueness of the Herman Miller Company is in its roots, and I can't help wondering whether those roots can remain healthy, in the light of changes at the other end of the growth process. That sounds pretty grim, and it could be; yet there is nothing sacred about roots as such. The world is full of companies that have been disconnected from their roots for so long that no one even remembers what they once were. Those companies may survive; many of them prosper. But, eventually, for sustenance they have to put down roots in some new place, necessarily becoming something else in the process.

Herman Miller has for several years been moving across the threshold of a radical new enterprise, most highly visible in the form of the Action Office and Co/Struc systems and the reorganization required to support them. It is worth asking whether that movement has torn, or will tear, the company from the roots in which it has found its vitality since the 1930s. To address the question we have to be very clear about what these roots are. It is easy to see where to look for them.

There is no way to discover or reveal the story of Herman Miller without considering the curious life of D. J. De Pree. This is not because De Pree "was" the company, in the sense that Watson "was" IBM. Some corporation heads have been so dominant as to leave little distinction between the man and the firm, but De Pree was not one of them. It's just that whatever uniqueness there is in the Herman Miller corporation stems directly from the unique combination of events and people whose influence he was open to.

The operative word is *open,* for De Pree was as much influenced as influence. His control

The Design of Herman Miller D. J. De Pree: The Roots

D. J. De Pree. Photograph by Terry Vande Water.

of the company did not lie merely in imposing his will on subordinates, although he did that of course. Rather it lay in his performance as selective conduit for the ideas of others. As it happened, these others were designers, and that made all the difference—it led to Herman Miller's hegemony in the field of design.

Of the 11 men De Pree regards as major influences in his life, four were designers: Gilbert Rohde, George Nelson, Charles Eames, and Robert Propst. Another, Carl Frost, is a management consultant with extremely strong ties to Herman Miller. Others include his sons, Hugh, Max, and John. The first two play roles of major influence at Herman Miller—Hugh as president and Max as chairman of the board.

Max De Pree remarks:

"There are two ways of competing in this business—you can nickel and dime the competition to death, or you can take giant steps that distinguish you from them. But the only way to take giant steps is to have giants. D. J.'s principal strength was the ability to abandon himself to the strength of unusual people. Of course we all know that one of the really important business skills is the ability to delegate, but D. J. went much further. Being abandoned to someone else's strength is a giant step that goes beyond delegation—that is when you get super performance from people."

It is somewhat embarrassing, at least for me, to write about a company in terms of the founder's religious convictions. But in this case it must be done. The point is not to claim a piety observable from the outside (there is no drinking at official Herman Miller functions, but that goes for IBM too and probably for the National Organization for the Reform of Marijuana Laws), but to show the impetus of a process from the inside.

For years Herman Miller intrigued me with its apparent incongruity. I kept viewing the company as a long-running soap opera that asked the question, "Can a small furniture manufacturer in the American Middle West find happiness with the world's most sophisticated designers?" The answer was plainly yes, but the question persisted rhetorically: How to reconcile the Dutch Reformed attitudes of the makers with the jet-set lifestyles of the people who bought the products?

As it turns out, no reconciliation is necessary. The Herman Miller product was the perfect amalgam of the square and the hip because of the recognition by both D. J. De Pree and the designers that the conflict was between styles and not values. As long as the design execution was based on values, there was curiously little conflict. The external expressions of old-time religion (no drinking, no smoking, grace before meat) had nothing to do with the furniture. But the belief in quality and honesty had a great deal to do with the furniture, for it could be, and was, shared by those who repudiated the Christian precepts, if they even acknowledged them at all. What brought Herman Miller to the avant-garde was an emphasis on problem solving that was congenial not only to both the Old and New Testaments but to Bauhaus declarations of principle as well. For good measure, the Reformed Calvinist concept of stewardship was extended to design.

Once I asked Tom Pratt, vice-president of marketing, how any company head could have taken the business risks De Pree had assumed in the name of honest contemporary design. The answer I got combines the insights of humanistic psychology with the kind of faith associated with radio broadcasts you hear while driving through Indianapolis on a Sunday morning. Here's what Pratt said:

"D. J. did feel the weight of other people. After all, his judgment affected other lives, and the willingness to risk does not mean irresponsibility. But Herman Miller was in such desperate circumstances that there was no alternative to taking risks. The company was failing, and it's the guy who's sickest that recognizes the healer.

"But there is more to it than that. D. J. was willing to take risks because of his conviction that divine guidance directs your steps. What looked like a business risk was really an investment of faith in a living God, and represented obedience to God's word. With faith like that, what look to others like monumental risks seem wholly secure to you.

"That security was reinforced by D. J.'s concept of significance, as stemming from the love of God and creation in His image. To base personal importance on performance alone was a humanistic, capitalistic view; and while that was the basic value system of the world D. J. was in, it certainly was not the value system on which *his* life was predicated.

"As a businessman, of course, he was part of the capitalistic system, and he saw his business role as the performance of service.

"But he also understood clearly the Biblical teaching of diligence—to 'do heartily as unto the Lord' whatever you put your hand to. From that standpoint, performance was the natural testimony, if you will, of a right relationship with God. It was not the preoccupation of your total being and was not the basis for significance in God's sight.

"Man was significant for who he was—that is, who he was in Christ, who had promised 'I will never leave you nor forsake you' and 'all things work together for good to them who love the Lord.' In that light, failure or risk of failure could never be catastrophic."

I didn't know how to handle an explanation like that, but the man it seeks to explain is, according to George Nelson, "as close to a Christian as anyone is likely to get."

At 84, D. J. De Pree is electric with an alert spirituality, an inner security that is in no way complacent. He talks with alacrity and good cheer about the afterlife, which is no less real to him than any other experience and to which he looks forward with enthusiasm. He expects it to be an improvement over this world —not that he has any quarrel with this one; it seems to him to work as it was intended to.

Within minutes of my first meeting with De Pree, we were talking not about Herman Miller but about the writings of a theologian named Elton Trueblood. Which is to say we *were* talking about Herman Miller, for more than 25 years ago Trueblood had written:

"The terrible danger of our time consists in the fact that ours is a *cut-flower civilization.* Beautiful as cut flowers may be, and much as we may use our ingenuity to keep them looking fresh for a while, they will eventually die, and they die because they are severed from their sustaining roots."

"Isn't that really a statement of the Herman Miller problem?" I asked D. J.

"Yes," he said.

Dirk Jan De Pree was born in 1891, one of three children fathered by a tinsmith who dabbled in Democratic politics. In 1909, just out of high school, D. J. got a job with the Michigan Star Furniture Company, doing general office work. Michigan Star had been formed four years before by a group of Zeeland businessmen, one of whom was Herman Miller. They converted a defunct canning factory to the manufacture of traditional furniture, chiefly Princess dressers, consisting of two drawers with an upright mirror. The sale of these dressers to Sears Roebuck was the company's principal business.

As a boy, D. J. had read deeply, if not widely. While the King James Bible was his major literary influence, he also turned for advice to the columns of *American Boy* magazine. As an adult, he continued to read both and also the *Sunday School Times.* One day he read a *Sunday School Times* article called, "How to Plan Your Day," and instantly began applying what he had learned. "That was simple enough," he explains, "because I had a clear knowledge of what needed to be done. After all, there was only the boss, a secretary, and me. I had to operate a typewriter, go into the factory to follow up orders, and so forth. I could control my time."

The time-saving tips worked so well that from then on De Pree was able to finish his day's work at the furniture company by noon. The rest of the time he studied accounting, not out of any great love for numbers, but because the income tax had begun in 1913 and he could see that new skills would be called for.

The Design of Herman Miller D. J. De Pree: The Roots

"I became extremely interested in cost accounting," De Pree says. "It was fascinating to break the business down into a lot of little businesses. For example, we had a coal-fire burner and some generators, so we were a power business. Since we owned the property we were a real estate business."

De Pree also began reading books by efficiency experts, an activity interesting in the light of Herman Miller Inc.'s later involvement in the management of office work. "The boss didn't like the idea of my spending all that time reading," De Pree says. "However, he did pay my expenses to an efficiency convention in Milwaukee. My reading of Frederick Taylor and the other time-management people began a lifetime of reading for me, hardly any of it for fun. That is, I hardly ever read novels."

In 1914, D. J. De Pree married Nellie Miller. While this was not a case of marrying the boss's daughter, it was later to become one. The majority of Michigan Star stockholders were, in De Pree's view, "neglectful," and in 1923 Herman Miller, Nellie's father, together with D. J. (using borrowed money) bought 51 percent of the stock. D. J. called on Jake Elenbaas, the principal stockholder, found him in his vegetable garden, and persuaded him to sell the rest of the stock to associates of Miller. Because he thought "Michigan Star" was corny, D. J. renamed the company after Herman Miller, who was never active in its operation, however.

"Mr. Miller set me on the quality trail," D. J. says today. "In 1923, we had moved from the Princess dressers to a bedroom suite that retailed for $1,000. Years later, when Bucky Fuller spent a day consulting with us (for a fee of $1,000), one of the things he talked about was the importance of making all prototypes of the best material and with the best workmanship. This was a policy we were already pursuing, and it started with Mr. Miller. It took three to four years for a product to be accepted, and a good design could go down the drain because of quality failure."

With the new name, the company began to put a new emphasis on quality and design, taking on the services of Edgar Somes, a "top freelance designer" in Grand Rapids. While this was a design improvement, probably almost anything would have been. It really was a matter of moving from no design to some design, or rather from inept copying to first-rate copying. After a time, Somes was succeeded by another Grand Rapids designer, Aurelio Bevelacqua, who also "designed" in the customary Grand Rapids manner, turning to books not for inspiration but for pictures to copy from. As a "good designer" he made the copies faithful to the original.

By the late twenties, competition in the furniture industry had become fierce. Department stores were trading down, and factories in the South were making inroads into markets that had previously been controlled from the Mid-

The Design of Herman Miller D. J. De Pree: The Roots

west. Herman Miller was not doing anything appreciably different or better than anyone else, and it was hard to see how that situation would ever change, pervaded as it was by what De Pree saw as "four major evils."

The first evil lay in the fact of a buyer's market. The second evil was that there were four distinct seasonal markets, *each* of them a buyer's market. The buyer's market created what De Pree identified as the third evil—the "ear-to-the-ground attitude" that dominated furniture manufacturing. Like all its competition, Herman Miller tried to get reliable tips on whatever arbitrary changes buyers were going to seek in their quest for novelty and then gear production accordingly. This meant that the industry was literally reactionary: it initiated nothing, but merely reacted to circumstances or rumors of circumstances. Companies had no control over design and factories had no control over what they made. Design and manufacturing were merely mechanical reactions to the stimuli called buyers.

Evil number four was that manufacturers had very little control over the selling of their products. Sales in the furniture industry were completely in the hands of individual contractors who worked on a 6 or 7 percent commission basis.

As if all that weren't bad enough, the Herman Miller Company was badly underfinanced. In 1930, looking around at the notoriously poor-paying furniture industry, De Pree saw nothing but evils. Looking ahead, he saw bankruptcy about a year away. There was no doubt in his mind that Herman Miller would not make it — not "as Herman Miller was then." But why should it stay as it was then? D. J. himself was changing. By this time "I had come to feel that my lot in life was to find a niche in which we could perform and no longer be a fabricator for brokers and buyers," he says. "That was the only plan I ever had."

But the evils remained. Unable to correct them, D. J. did the next best thing: he prayed.

The Design of Herman Miller

D. J. De Pree: The Roots

Company's first products were ornate period residential furniture, indistinguishable from the products of other Grand Rapids area manufacturers.

Prayer, God, Jesus Christ, and certain of the disciples are as tangible to D. J. De Pree as Eames chairs, and he has a habit of speaking about them in the same way. Trying to associate a date with a new factory or a new sales manager, he will say, "Let's see, that was just about the time I came face to face with the Triune God." This kind of thing could be disconcerting, but somehow isn't. I don't know why it isn't.

Was D. J.'s prayer answered directly? Not with an immediate response. But in the summer of 1930, a man named Gilbert Rohde walked into the company's Grand Rapids showroom and introduced De Pree to the subject of modern furniture — "A subject about which I understood little or nothing," De Pree says. (The company did have experience in *moderne,* though, which they began making in small quantities after De Pree had seen an exhibition of French furniture design.)

There was a word for Rohde's unexpected, unsolicited appearance and D. J. knew the word: *providential.* Having been certain that nothing short of a miracle could save Herman Miller, he was just as certain that Rohde was bringing in the miracle or at least could be commissioned to perform it.

Providential or not, Rohde's arrival had sprung from a routine motive: he had come to Grand Rapids to sell his designs and was not having an easy time of it. De Pree was aware of that: "I imagine we were pretty far down on his list, but nobody else would listen to him."

Rohde's designs for other companies ended in closeouts, according to Jimmy Eppinger, a Herman Miller salesman during that period and later sales manager, who adds, "*All* of the *art moderne* designs in the late twenties were closeouts. Publicists for the fashion industry and people like that would go to Europe on department store business assignments and come back with modern fashions in furniture. But the trouble was that nobody believed in contemporary furniture. The forms were unacceptable and they were not accepted."

Most of Rohde's experience had been acquired in his work as an advertising and display illustrator. But he impressed De Pree particularly with his assertion that although he had not designed much furniture, he was a "student of living." "I know how people live," Rohde told D. J., "and I know how they are going to live. Modern living calls for smaller houses with lower ceilings, and this in turn calls for a different kind of furniture."

Could Rohde design such furniture?

He said he could.

Would he design such furniture for Herman Miller?

Yes. His fee would be $1,000 per group. (The Grand Rapids designers Herman Miller was

The Design of Herman Miller Early Growth: Rohde

One of Gilbert Rohde's major contributions, as these residential and office designs of his indicate, was to strip away excess weight and decoration.

using, the most expensive in their class, were charging $300 per group at that time. Others got $100 per group, and for that fee the designer not only provided detailed drawings but selected the wood and supervised the installation at the market.) In the end, they settled on a royalty arrangement of 3 percent because Herman Miller didn't have the cash to pay Rohde's fee.

That was the beginning of a design adventure that would carry the name and the products of this obscure little company across the world. In the United States only IBM, and in Europe only Olivetti and Braun, connoted design excellence in the way Herman Miller came to connote it.

Rohde's first Herman Miller project replaced the ornate, high-priced seven-piece bedroom suite that was the company's staple. Arguing that modern homes had neither foot space nor need for such a suite, he designed a substitute consisting of four basic large pieces.

When D. J. saw the first drawings he was unhappy. "I couldn't imagine that a chest of drawers shouldn't stand on a turned post," he says. But Rohde was not only eliminating the turned posts, he was reducing the amount of wood and using plastics.

D. J. politely wrote to Rohde, protesting that the pieces were too plain, needed surface enrichment, and looked like something done in a high school manual training class. Rohde politely replied that Herman Miller didn't have to make the furniture, but if they did make it his designs had to be produced as they were, with no changes.

D. J. agreed, but still feared that the furniture was too stark to sell. However, it did sell from the beginning. Ludwig-Baumann, a large New York installment house, bought 12 of the sets.

Jimmy Eppinger remembers:

"What Herman Miller had been making was carved, painted, marble-topped case goods — ostentatious beyond belief, but all hand-crafted and difficult to make. The main market had been Lower East Side merchants and wholesale showrooms, but that market disappeared with the crash. D. J. tried to copy Jamestown style — volume-priced furniture that was higher in quality and price than the Southern style, but lower than Grand Rapids. Then he turned to the classics—Chippendale, a modified Sheraton, maybe something French.

"The fact that the Rohde designs were unadorned fit D. J.'s notion of Christian sincerity. He must have hated all that other stuff. Of course he knew nothing about design to start with, but he was self-taught."

"I came to see that the starting point of our design had been immoral," De Pree says now. It was immoral chiefly in its pretense, but that pretense hid other immoralities: moldings and carvings were used to conceal sins of sloppy workmanship, for instance. "With his simplicity, Rohde had taken away our means of covering up," De Pree realized. "We had to learn new manufacturing techniques, such as how to make mitered joints in a very precise way."

"There was a parallel simplicity in De Pree's personal lifestyle," Eppinger recalls. "He had a family of nine and crammed them all into a Ford that anyone could see was too small for the purpose. In 1933, he was offered a fabulous trade-in deal on a Chrysler that was exactly what he needed. He couldn't bring himself to buy it though, because he thought that back in Zeeland it would look ostentatious."

"Rohde was beginning to teach me such wonderful things," D. J. reports. "One of his teachings was, 'You're not making furniture anymore. You're providing a way of life.'" De Pree took that seriously enough to perceive where the obstacles lay. "I realized," he says, "that it was a great opportunity. But I was learning that we had to get closer to the ultimate user."

"D. J. said *that*?" a marketing man asks. "If he realized it then, how come we're still having to learn it today?"

Closeness to the ultimate user is not the only contemporary design concept introduced at Herman Miller in the 1930s. "Rohde introduced the idea of modern storage spaces," De Pree claims, "with a concern for increasing value by saving space and increasing storage capacity. He invented the sectional sofa. Also, from the beginning, Rohde had the systems idea of duplicating the same piece. EOG—Rohde's Executive Office Group—had 15 components, out of which 400 things could be made!"

The ideas were all valid and all very hard to sell. In the late 1930s, when he developed EOG, Rohde was trying to find a manufacturer. De Pree suggested Herman Miller, but Rohde protested: "You're having enough trouble paying my royalties as it is." He tried manufacturers in New York, Boston, and Iowa, but he still couldn't sell the line. Finally, De Pree said, "Why don't you at least let us make samples? Then you'll have an easier time selling it." But Rohde couldn't sell the samples either, and in the end Herman Miller manufactured the line.

"When Rohde appeared," Eppinger recalls, "he had no audience and needed Miller. Miller had no line and needed Rohde. That was D. J.'s vision. A modest, conservative man, as D. J. was, doesn't generally take the kind of risk he took, but he was willing to gamble. To hedge the bet, he also hired Frieda Diamond to design the company's traditional line. Frieda's gift was to contemporize the accepted — Chippendale, eighteenth-century

English, knotty pine." When the WPA produced an index of American design, it included some Shaker designs, and based on that, Frieda Diamond brought out a Shaker line for Herman Miller.

"Remember," Eppinger says, "that when Rohde came to Herman Miller all the company made was case goods. Rohde introduced seating, which they had no experience in manufacturing. Like all wood factories, they resisted everything that wasn't wood. Upholstery and metal were farmed out."

By 1934, Rohde had gotten the company into the upholstery business. "We were now making everything but kitchen furniture," De Pree says, "but I still don't know how we were paying for it. We were an undercapitalized company."

Undercapitalized though they were, that year Herman Miller took extra space in the Keeler Building in Grand Rapids and displayed a full Rohde section and a full Frieda Diamond section, like a company unsure of what it wanted to be when it grew up. The same year, Jimmy Eppinger, then the East Coast salesman, occupied a desk in Rohde's studio in order to learn about modern furniture, the first step toward establishing an important Herman Miller principle: design innovation requires innovative merchandising techniques, and these in turn require that salesmen understand the design. In 1934, Wanamaker's had 12 sample rooms of Rohde and Diamond furniture in their New York store and 13 rooms in their Philadelphia store. Eppinger managed to get Rohde's assistant, Elizabeth Kaufer, a job in the store's decorating department, taking charge of the display rooms. "She was the only one there who understood anything about the furniture," he explains.

"I had 80 furniture salesmen at Wanamaker's," Ms. Kaufer remembers. "I gave them a course in what contemporary furniture was and how to sell it."

The scheme was hugely successful, with the New York inventory turning over 12 times that year. The Philadelphia experiment failed, however, which D. J. attributes to an unsympathetic, even hostile, buyer. "We could see the need of eventually bypassing department stores that had such attitudes," he says. "We decided to get into the showroom business as soon as we could."

Why was contemporary furniture generally so hard to sell? For one thing, it looked funny. For another, it was so simple looking that it raised the question, "How can it be worth the price?" Perhaps an even more important reason was that the people who liked it didn't necessarily know how to use it. People would look at the new line, like it, agree that it made sense, but still object. They would ask, "How can we put a sectional sofa in a place where we have always had a sofa and two chairs?"

"Our own salesmen initially were all the broker type," D. J. recalls. "They were 5 percent, 6 percent, 7 percent men with other lines to sell. They weren't interested in our Rohde line, because to sell it they would have to understand it. They were all highly intelligent men, but unaccustomed to bringing their intelligence into sales talk in the way the new line required. Their sales approach depended a great deal on friendship and entertaining and status, not on the real hard, intelligent selling of things that would help people."

The need for that kind of intelligence at Herman Miller is far more important today, with concepts like Action Office and Co/-Struc, than it was in Rohde's day.

"All our lives at Herman Miller, we have really been teaching planning," Max De Pree says. "The early planning was not unlike the planning necessary to sell Action Office, which is really an expansion of the kinds of programs that Eppinger set up in the thirties. Whenever there is an innovation, there has to be some explanation of how to take advantage of it. Eppinger, of course, was working at something far more difficult than just teaching the users how to use the furniture. He was teaching the buyers how to sell it, and in that role was a key figure in the contemporary furniture industry."

But the design program had to be sold within the company before it could be sold *by* the company. Eppinger himself notes: "D. J. De Pree was solely responsible for acceptance of the design program. He had the vision and he implemented it."

Early catalog featured modular desk system.

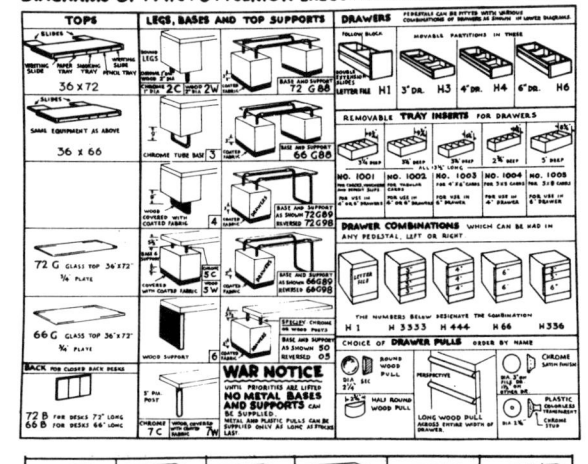

The Design of Herman Miller   The Flowering of Design

Gilbert Rohde died in 1944, leaving Herman Miller with a design commitment but no designer. The company at that time had three salesmen, and D. J. turned to them for suggestions. One prospect was the German architect Eric Mendelssohn; another was industrial designer Russell Wright. The following year D. J. found a successor, in providential fashion. Intrigued by an article in *Architectural Forum* proposing that walls be used for storage, he called Jimmy Eppinger in New York and asked him to contact the author. When Eppinger called *Forum* and asked to speak to the author, he was told that there were two: Henry Wright and George Nelson, who were the magazine's managing editors. Eppinger asked for Wright, who suggested he talk to Nelson.

The talk was productive from the beginning. "George said he knew nothing about furniture design, but would love to do it," Eppinger recalls. "Then he began talking about what needed to be done. He was the first one who really said the kind of thing we were hoping someone would say."

As it happened, Nelson was on his way to Detroit for a meeting, and an appointment with D. J. was set up. They met in a hotel restaurant and spent an evening talking about religion. Each was horrified by what the other believed about the Bible, although for Nelson the shock was softened by a steady stream of martinis. For D. J. the shock was softened by an admiration for "George's fertile mind, his design awareness, and his ability to articulate important principles, some of which we were already unconsciously practicing."

George Nelson's impact on the company was enormous. Herman Miller and Rohde had needed each other out of mutual desperation. Herman Miller and Nelson needed each other because each had achieved a certain measure of success but was seeking new directions. Nelson had described bold design ideas that he had not yet executed. Herman Miller had assumed an attitude toward modern furniture that it had expressed in only a very limited way.

As design director, Nelson did far more than direct design. He supplied the company with a corporate philosophy; he formulated a marketing strategy — for example, identifying architects, rather than department store buyers, as the people most likely to be sympathetic to Herman Miller products; he helped salespeople; he wrote frequent, relentlessly honest assessments of what the company was doing.

He also served as corporate tutor, stimulator of meetings, peripatetic teacher of design and marketing. Sometimes he was called to Zeeland for nothing more than a day or two of walking around the plant and talking to people, an activity the De Prees regard as significant, if not measurable, in its effect.

The Design of Herman Miller

The Flowering of Design

In 1947, Nelson published a major survey of the American furniture industry in *Fortune* magazine. One of his colleagues remarks: "George wrote that round-up article not just for *Fortune* but for himself. He had just got a new job, and here was the chance to talk to leaders in the furniture industry, survey the industry's methods, and incorporate what he had learned into the design of his own furniture."

The *Fortune* article was not flattering to furniture manufacturers. It described the industry as scattered and fragmented and the product as "endlessly and unnecessarily varied, and almost uniformly uninspired," and Grand Rapids manufacturers in particular were angered by it. It didn't make them feel any better to learn that the author was about to become Herman Miller's director of design.

On the basis of his survey, Nelson prepared a paper telling Herman Miller what to do. For example, one thing he told them to do was to standardize whenever there was no reason not to, pointing out that each of the 24 bedroom sets in the line had different drawers.

Another recommendation that Nelson calmly lodged with the company had to do with volume: "If we're going to do the things we say we want to do, then we have to generate enough cash to do them. You have to become a $2 million company."

"I had no vision about gross at that time," D. J. says. "I thought of us as a $400,000 company." (Last year's total worldwide sale of Herman Miller products was $60 million.)

There is a Herman Miller myth to the effect that the company was shaped by design. The myth is no myth, but it would be more accurate to say that the company was shaped by *designers*. Design to D. J. was an extension of the designer, the essence of a man, and therefore a sacred trust. This realization called for a design custodianship. If the designer worked in an atmosphere of potential, the company was responsible for realizing that potential. Once you accepted a design, D. J. believed, you had to treat it as a commitment; he believed further that once you accepted a designer you were almost equally committed to whatever he designed. Since there was never any way of knowing in advance what that would be, Herman Miller stood ready to produce goods with materials and processes in which it had no competence or experience—a state of affairs that made quality control extremely difficult.

Yet quality control was basic to the concept. "The designer deserves the best we can do for him," D. J. would say, meaning too that the consumer deserved the best-made product. Management, therefore, was obliged to get it to him: part of design custodianship was the innovative selling required to follow through on the manufacturing commitment.

A man who sees a designer in terms of Providence is likely to see a product in terms of

Stewardship — not a gift outright but something entrusted to your care for dissemination. In the thirties, D. J. had regarded independent broker salesmen, handling many competitive lines, as an evil. In the seventies, he regards it as evil to permit salesmen to decide what they will sell, for it runs counter to top management's exercise of its responsibility.

Pointing to an Eames molded plywood chair, D. J. says, "That's beautiful, comfortable, easy to move. It's unimprovable. It's a national treasure that ought to be made available." In his evangelical zeal, he is reminiscent of the missionaries who put Mother Hubbards on south sea island natives whether they wanted them or not. Charles Eames says fondly, "There was a time when D. J. wanted to get every Hottentot into a molded plywood chair."

"If you own a piece of land," D. J. feels, "you are responsible for farming it. In the same way, if you have taken on a design, you are responsible for selling it up to its full potential. We shouldn't drop anything prematurely, but we have — the Eames Contract System, George's day bed...."

De Pree's Biblical aversion to materialism did not preclude a deep respect for *things*. Nelson had described each product as loaded with "impounded energy" that must be factored into the costing. D. J. seized on the concept and applied it to the entire company and to life generally. ("The Bible," he observes, "has more impounded energy than any other book.")

No American designer writes better than George Nelson or thinks more clearly about what he writes, and this talent was more than incidental to his success at Herman Miller; he was able to define the company for itself and its public with breathtaking lucidity.

A case in point is the 1948 catalog, which was a new departure for Herman Miller and for manufacturing corporations in general. Knowing that the fresh new designs would be copied, Nelson reasoned in effect: if ripoff is inevitable, why not lie back and enjoy it? Or, better yet, exploit it. The catalog included all the dimensions of the furniture, making it that much easier to copy. It was his idea to *sell* the catalog, as if it were a book on design. And since Nelson was its author, it *was* a book on design, and a first-rate one.

In the foreword, Nelson describes Herman Miller as a company unremarkable in every respect but one: "its philosophy—an attitude so deeply felt that to the best of my knowledge it has never been formulated." Nelson then went on to formulate it. He wrote:

"The attitude that governs Herman Miller's behavior, as far as I can make out, is compounded of the following set of principles.

"*What you make is important.* Herman Miller, like all other companies, is governed by the

The Design of Herman Miller   The Flowering of Design

George Nelson extended Rohde's perception that new living and working styles required corresponding furniture design. His BSC (Basic Storage Components) included freestanding residential modules and L-shaped desk.

The Design of Herman Miller The Flowering of Design

The Design of Herman Miller The Flowering of Design

Nelson's wall storage systems introduced an unprecedented versatility to the market.

rules of the American economy, but I have yet to see quality of construction or finish skimped to meet a popular price bracket, or for any other reason.

"*Design is an integral part of the business.* The designer's decisions are as important as those of the sales or production departments. If the design is changed, it is with the designer's participation and approval. There is no pressure on him to modify to meet the market.

"*The product must be honest.* Herman Miller discontinued production of period reproductions almost 12 years ago because its designer, Gilbert Rohde, had convinced the management that imitation of traditional designs was insincere esthetically. (I couldn't believe this story when I first heard it, but after my experience of the past two years, I know it is true.)

"*You decide what you will make.* Herman Miller has never done any market research or any pretesting of its products to determine what the market 'will accept.' If designer and management like a solution to a particular furniture problem, it is put into production. There is no attempt to conform to the so-called norms of 'public taste,' nor any special faith in the methods used to evaluate the 'buying public.'

"*There is a market for good design.* This assumption has been more than confirmed, but it took a great deal of courage to make it and stick to it."

The 1948 book—a record of furniture in production — was both a specification catalog and a reference work for professionals and students. It sold so well at $5 that the company was able to price a second edition at $10. An effective promotional device internationally, the catalog confirmed Nelson's conviction that (1) it would have value as a book, (2) if it did, it ought to be sold, and (3) the fact that it was sold would in itself increase its value.

With the momentum Rohde had given the company, Herman Miller and Nelson became locked into what might be called a precious circle. The company had already begun to put into practice what Nelson was better able to articulate than anyone else. And after it was described, the company became better at putting it into practice. Nelson's verbal fluency paved the way for his design fluency in relationship to both Herman Miller and the market.

"It was the climate," Jimmy Eppinger recalls, "and that was largely D. J.'s doing. In a climate like that, everyone sings: George sang, Eames sang, I sang." Nelson's singing took the form of a superb first collection incorporating the kinds of ideas he had heretofore only written about—a headboard that tilted so you could lean against it and read, a coffee table with a tray that lifted out, and a version of the storage wall that had first brought him to De Pree's attention.

Nelson had identified architects and decorators as the logical group to reach. Herman Miller was ready to reach them. De Pree and Eppinger were pioneers in selling contemporary furniture and contributed to the popularity of the decorator showroom. Designers take such showrooms for granted now, but they were rare in the thirties.

In 1938, the Merchandise Mart in Chicago was eager for tenants. Eppinger argued that there would be nothing to lose in moving the Herman Miller showroom from Grand Rapids to Chicago. As an inducement, the Merchandise Mart offered to let Herman Miller keep their doors open between markets, which meant they were no longer confined to four markets a year and were accessible to architects.

"The showroom business was sub rosa in those days," he says. "Remember that the architect didn't even appear in the picture at that time — it was considered unethical even to talk to an architect. If we didn't sell through standard distributors and furniture stores, we were ostracized."

Yet standard distributors were hopelessly ill-equipped to understand the product. And those who were equipped were off limits. "The device that circumvented the system was called 'wholesale trade,' " Eppinger explains, "and that's what really created the showroom."

If the new road to the market wasn't paved with gold, it did offer unexpected financial advantages. The standard trade discount was 50 and 10. "But," the still-ebullient Eppinger points out, "the trade could sell to designers and decorators at a 40 percent discount. This meant that the company got 60 percent of its price, as opposed to 45 percent."

As discounts went down, Eppinger's commissions went up accordingly, for he controlled the showroom at that time. Herman Miller paid the rent, but Eppinger (who did not become a Herman Miller employee until 1953) paid for the operation, and the showroom staff was on his payroll, not the company's. "That system worked because the De Prees wanted it to," he says.

There were still other advantages to the showroom business: the cash flow leaped dramatically because, unlike department store and distributor sales, each showroom sale yielded one third in cash!

"But remember that *none of this was by plan*," Eppinger asserts — a theme repeated by all three De Prees. "It came about because the orthodox channels of distribution were not hospitable. Although I initiated the showroom setup, I didn't do it because of cash-flow advantage. I didn't know that would happen, and

The Design of Herman Miller   **The Flowering of Design**

The coffee tables and writing desk are examples of Nelson's elegance. The glass table, designed by sculptor Isamu Noguchi, is an example of Nelson's imaginative recruiting of design talent. Photographs of tables by Ezra Stoller.

The Design of Herman Miller The Flowering of Design

Nelson's 1954 chaise longue.

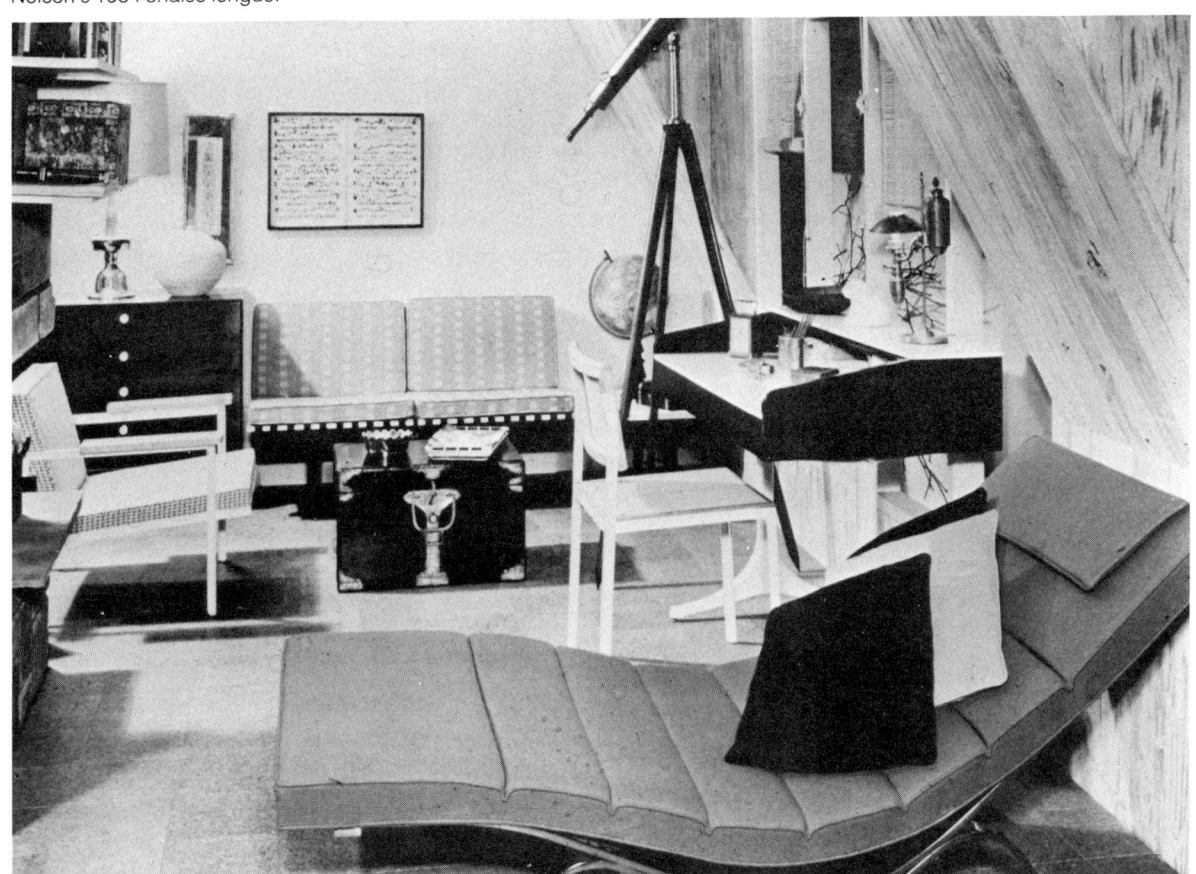

The Design of Herman Miller   The Flowering of Design

Sling sofa designed by Nelson suspends leather cushions in a sling of neoprene within a chrome steel frame.

The Design of Herman Miller The Flowering of Design

Nelson's aluminum-based office seating incorporates human factors data into its solution.

in Zeeland they didn't even know what cash flow meant. Herman Miller had a CPA only to prepare year-end reports until my CPA insisted that they get better accounting guidance. The books in Zeeland were kept by D. J.'s sister — who was a pretty good bookkeeper by the way."

The company today has showrooms in Chicago, Los Angeles, and Washington, D. C., and sales offices in other cities. Although a great deal of selling is done by Herman Miller people both in the showrooms and the field, actual orders are handled only by stocking dealers. The showroom's function is exposure and information, the latter especially important because so many of the company's products have design features that are not apparent on the surface. The dealer's function—in addition to selling —is installation and follow-through, including service.

The architect and designer, then, have been supplanted by the dealer as the sole direct buyer; the traditional showroom principle, however, remains the same — serving the customer by cutting the middleman in rather than out.

Nelson's early designs were compatible enough with Rohde's, and the transition was enhanced by Nelson's hiring one of Rohde's designers, Ernest Farmer. Since De Pree and the company generally were already committed to contemporary furniture, Nelson could put his energies into building rather than proselytizing. In his 20 years as director of design, he created a procession of design innovations that captured the attention of the design world even if they didn't always capture the market. The best known of these are a day bed; a slat bench; a residential desk, which attracted the attention of architects who specified it for office use; a sensuous line of miniature cabinets, handmade by Zeeland craftsman who specialized in them; the thin-edge case group; the steel-frame cases; modular seating; the "marshmallow sofa"; the "coconut chair"; the comprehensive storage system; the sling sofa; and the catenary chair.

The most profitable of Nelson's ideas were not always carried to fruition by Herman Miller. "What we designed became best sellers," Nelson observes, "but they were always made best sellers by other manufacturers who knocked them off, not by Herman Miller. In our way, though, we were keeping America beautiful."

To implement the ideal that "the product must be made unassailable in the marketplace," Nelson and Charles Eames recommended that Herman Miller set up a Technical Center, like the one that General Motors had just established in Detroit.

"If only we had done it in the depth they wanted," D. J. laments. "But we didn't. And by not doing it we missed out on one of the greatest opportunities George ever presented us with — the Middle Management Group."

MMG was a line of wood, steel, and Micarta desks designed to give the company a broader market than was possible with Rohde's Executive Office Group. Dependent upon outside fabricators, Herman Miller had the steel parts made by a manufacturer of kitchen furniture. The arrangement was unworkable both technically (the manufacturer couldn't adjust his techniques to desks) and economically (joint manufacture meant a double profit margin). MMG was soon dropped from the line.

"But the principle of incorporating architectural detailing and color into desks was correct," D. J. says, "and it was proven correct by Steelcase, General Fireproofing, and others. We had failed to make the product unassailable in the marketplace, but George made a tremendous contribution to the steel furniture industry."

George Nelson's design influence in Herman Miller went beyond the vitality of his own designs. He brought in such other designers as Paul Lazlo and sculptor Isamu Noguchi. But far and away the most significant infusion of new design talent came with the introduction of Charles Eames to Herman Miller in 1946, shortly after Nelson joined the company.

In 1940, Eames and the architect Eero Saarinen had jointly won a first prize in the Museum of Modern Art's Organic Design competition for their molded plywood chairs. In the intervening years, Eames and his wife, Ray, had experimented with wood-molding techniques. They had, in 1942, been commissioned by the Navy to develop lightweight leg splints, which were manufactured by the Evans Products Company in Venice, California. That project gave the Eameses access to molding technology developed by the British for mosquito bombers. Through their own assiduous research, Charles and Ray developed some chairs that more than fulfilled the promise of the competition chairs.

Nelson himself had been working on a chair along similar lines. When he saw the Eames chairs, he threw out the kraft-paper models he had been developing. "These are three to five years ahead of our own," he told D. J. and Eppinger. As a result, Eames was sought as consultant designer, although he was already under contract to Evans for the plywood chairs.

Eames and the furniture he designed are famous. What is not so well known is the kind of company-designer relationship the furniture grew out of, a relationship described by a Herman Miller executive as "not a contractual marriage, but a covenantal marriage." At the time his friend George Nelson was recommending Eames to Herman Miller, Charles and Ray Eames had become the Molded Plywood Division of the Evans Products

Company; and in the Venice, California, shop that was to become their headquarters for more than 30 years they were continuing their experiments in molding and bonding techniques. They developed not only new chairs but the "KZAM! machines" to make them with, so called by the Eameses because KZAM! was the noise they made in the last stage of the process.

The resultant chairs represented so radical an advance in furniture design that the Museum of Modern Art in 1946 installed a small exhibition called "New Furniture Designed by Charles Eames"—the museum's first one-man furniture show. (In 1973, MOMA held a large retrospective survey of his work.) The 1946 exhibit, which Eames designed, included a motion-picture display showing the transfer of energy from the seat of the chair to the leg. Even then, his impulse was to communicate process.

Eppinger still remembers the excitement and despair of his visit to the MOMA show. "As I'm leaving, Eames is still there monkeying with the exhibit. He doesn't know me, I don't know him. I look at the stuff. I'm sick. Nelson was right . . . this guy was five years ahead of us."

Later that evening, he was less sick, having learned by accident that Evans was looking for a furniture manufacturer to make the chairs. A few days later, D. J. De Pree and Eppinger met with Evans and made a deal.

If D. J., Nelson, and Eppinger loved the chair at first sight, Mr. Herman Miller's response was no less instantaneous. Reflecting his Grand Rapids background, Miller announced, "That's never going to go into any showroom that has my name on it!"

For a time it looked as if he were going to be right about that. The old canning factory was already strained beyond its capacity, with no room for the KZAM! machines. Perched at one end of a high-wire act that would make international design history, the Herman Miller Company was unable to take the first step.

They didn't have to. Mr. Evans had had second thoughts, and D. J. was able to wire Eppinger: A MOST PROVIDENTIAL THING HAS HAPPENED STOP EVANS WANTS TO MANUFACTURE THE CHAIRS FOR US STOP. . . . A new agreement was drawn up, relieving Herman Miller of any manufacturing responsibilities—Evans had actually bought a factory before the deal was settled—but leaving Herman Miller the marketing and distribution rights.

Two years later, Herman Miller was able to buy the manufacturing rights as well. They improved the quality and lowered the price, but not enough to satisfy either D. J. or Charles Eames. "We intended it to retail at $15," D. J. says. "I worked very hard to find a way to get the chair down to that price, but we never did."

The Design of Herman Miller The Flowering of Design

Early plywood furniture by Charles and Ray Eames included chairs for children.

The Design of Herman Miller

The Flowering of Design

Today people speak of "the Eames chair" as if the term were a single word describing a single chair. Most commonly they are referring to one of the molded plywood chairs or to the leather-covered lounge chair with ottoman or to the plastic shell chair.

Eames's distinction in furniture design is so well documented — not just in design literature and museum collections but in what seems like all the homes, offices, airports, and prestige advertising of our lives — that it has threatened to obscure his equal distinction in other forms of design problem solving. Yet the exhibits and films produced by the Eames office are spectacular achievements in the handling of ideas, including advanced scientific ideas. It is interesting that at a recent banquet held in honor of George Nelson and Charles and Ray Eames, the American Institute of Interior Designers paid tribute to the general contributions of the Eameses, rather than to their interior design contributions as such. Their citation reads:

"For expressing, in design, ideas that are personal and American at the same time they are public and international.

"For bringing to design the quality of thinking associated with the sciences, and for bringing to science the kind of imagination associated with design, and for showing us that they are inescapably part of the same process.

"For changing the way people sit, store things, build, play, communicate, teach, learn, and think."

As for furniture, the Herman Miller–Eames affiliation has produced the molded plywood chair, the molded plastic chair, the lounge chair and ottoman, the aluminum group, the soft-pad group, the wire chair, the compact sofa, the special chairs for Time-Life, Inc. and La Fonda del Sol, the tandem sling seating, the tandem shell seating, and a variety of other furniture products and systems.

"Systems implications are basic to Eames designs," says Bob Blaich, vice-president in charge of design and development. "For example, a molded fiberglass shell works equally well on its own four-leg pedestal base or on a tandem base. This systems effect was a key factor in our ability to move from residential to institutional design." In the sixties, an Eames-designed system of shells, castings, and arm surfaces was used in lecture halls on all State University of New York campuses.

Another system, the tandem sling seating, which may be Charles Eames's most often seen design, if not his most widely known one, was a specific project solution that has become generalized into an industry standard.

Harvey Stubsjoen, project designer for the interiors at Chicago's O'Hare airport, had prepared a seating program that was both comprehensive in its analysis and simple in its list of constraints. "As it turned out," Stubsjoen wrote in the November 1962 *Progressive Architecture*, "Eames had been thinking along the lines of developing public seating based on the concept of suspended upholstery, and was happy to continue in this direction." (The pattern of being asked to consider a project for which he already happens to have part of the solution is not unprecedented for Eames. His powerful film *Powers of Ten* was responsive to the needs of the Commission on College Physics, the client; but, in fact, Eames had been thinking and talking and sketching about the film for years before the commission approached him.)

Not all Eames designs have been market successes. One that wasn't — Eames Contract Storage system (ECS) — was among Herman Miller's earliest ventures into the educational market. ECS was a system of components that could be shipped knocked down, assembled right in the dormitory room, and wall attached—a requirement under federal funding regulations and useful as a way to keep students from stealing parts.

It was a case of precisely the right product at precisely the wrong time. Bob Blaich had spent a year talking to people about the problem. Eames produced a system that was inexpensive, used space (including vertical space) efficiently, and could be expected to materially enhance student life. That made it the right product.

It was the wrong time because the kind of student life the system enhanced was about to vanish. "Eames had the answer," Blaich says. "There was no doubt about it. The trouble was, the question had been set aside." The general student dissatisfaction of the late fifties was leading naturally to the desire of students to control their own environment and to live where and with whom they wanted.

D. J. is still astonished at Nelson's generosity in bringing other designers into the company to share his credits and his royalties. He was particularly astonished by Nelson's relinquishing his rights of approval in the case of Eames. For his part, Eames has no hesitation in attributing the company's overall design strength to Nelson.

"We got in a few licks, but essentially it was George," he says. "Actually, though, Herman Miller had an identity long before George got into it. In 1938, when I was working with Eliel Saarinen, I was contracting and specifying all the furniture for the Kleinhans Music Hall in Buffalo. There were three companies that stood out as making stuff we could use: Dunbar, Heywood-Wakefield, and Herman Miller. In the end, I designed a chair that Heywood made."

The Design of Herman Miller   The Flowering of Design

48

Among the collector's items in this Eames grouping is the folding plywood screen with canvas joints, made by Herman Miller in the forties.

The Design of Herman Miller The Flowering of Design

Eames Storage Units are a lightweight modular system of steel and plastic-coated plywood units.

The Design of Herman Miller The Flowering of Design

Eames vinyl-edged shell chair with wire base and Eames unupholstered wire chair with wire strut base.

The Design of Herman Miller   The Flowering of Design

Eames fiberglass-reinforced plastic office seating with loose-cushion upholstery.

The Design of Herman Miller   The Flowering of Design

The Design of Herman Miller The Flowering of Design

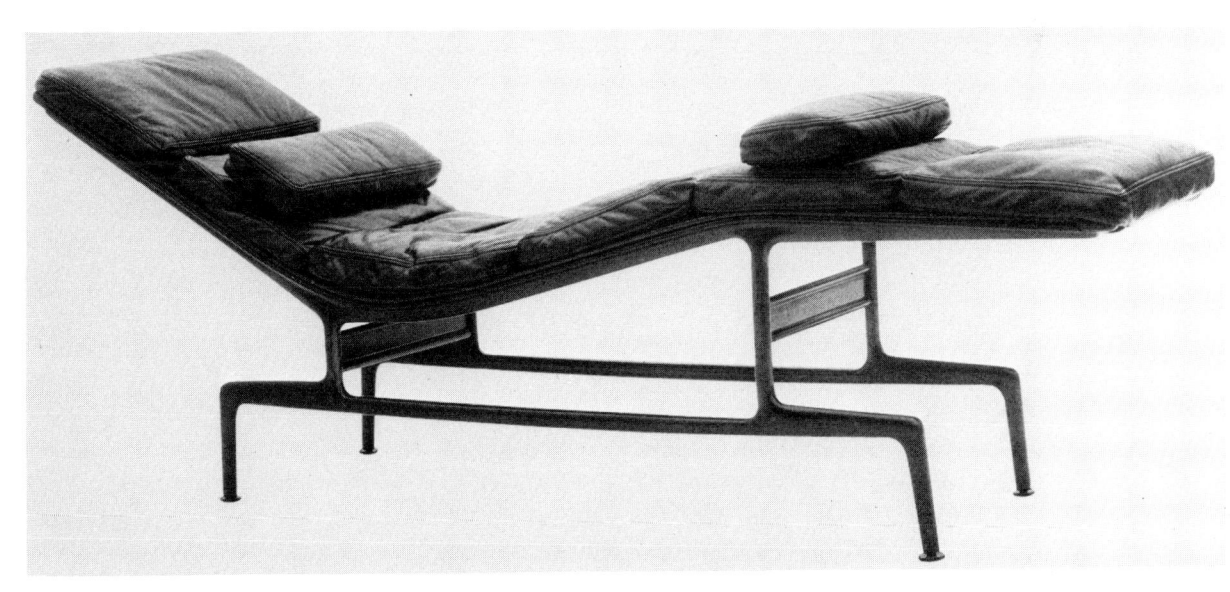

Eames narrow chaise has nylon-coated aluminum frame supporting six cushions zippered to each other. Two loose cushions provide further support and comfort. Soft pad chair, on Eames Universal base and frame, features double-stitched leather, dacron-filled pads. Comparison with molded plywood chair (opposite) illustrates both the diversity and the unity of his work over the years.

The Design of Herman Miller   The Flowering of Design

Stacking version of Eames shell extends the chair's usefulness to easily stored multiple seating.

The Design of Herman Miller The Flowering of Design

Eames tandem sling seating, designed for Chicago's O'Hare Airport, has become a staple in airports and other public areas all over the world.

The Design of Herman Miller The Flowering of Design

Herman Miller executives today look back in wonder (as who does not?) at the policy that whatever George Nelson and Charles Eames designed, Herman Miller made.

Was that really the way it was?

"Well, I had a constraint," Eames says, "a feeling that I didn't want to do anything that would get those nice people in trouble. Whatever happened with the Herman Miller Company and us came from taking the kind of risks no one would, or could, take today. But D. J. had a very useful business skill—a capacity for permitting only certain ideas to get through. And Jimmy Eppinger was able to interpret the Herman Miller position. In the early days Eppinger was our chief contact, transmitting enthusiasm between Zeeland and our office. Because of his ability to describe furniture needs to us, it never really was a matter of the company's being obligated to make anything we happened to design—although it looked that way."

Product designers whose work is commercially successful but not otherwise honored tend to scoff at design awards and museums. "The marketplace is the only museum I design for," is the common defense, delivered petulantly and usually followed by, "Art museums don't boost my client's products." It is true that museums have not much advanced the cause of washing machine manufacturers, but they have raised the sights of the furniture industry.

A case in point was the Museum of Modern Art's 1940 competition for modern furniture, which first brought Eames and Eero Saarinen to public attention. Organized by Eliot Noyes —with the help of Ira Hirshman, a Bloomingdale's executive who marshaled support from a number of department stores—the competition was juried by Alvar Aalto, Marcel Breuer, Alfred Barr, Edward Stone, and Frank Parish, a technical expert from Heywood-Wakefield. Noyes then produced and installed the Organic Design show based on the competition results.

In 1948, Hirshman got a group of installment furniture houses to sponsor an "International Competition for Low-Cost Furniture Design," intended to find new designers who could fill the manufacturing gap left by the war years. That competition was also held at the Museum of Modern Art and was directed by Edgar Kaufmann, Jr., who had succeeded Noyes as director of industrial design.

Out in Venice, Charles and Ray Eames were experimenting with glass-reinforced plastics, heretofore used for making lightweight radar domes. For the museum competition, however, Eames submitted a series of chair designs in stamped sheet metal. The chairs shared second prize for seating.

"We were interested in a plastic chair," Eames says, "but the technology at the time made that seem very difficult. We even made some drawings in aluminum, but finally chose sheet metal because of the highly advanced mass production techniques available for it, especially in stamped parts. Also, Neoprene coating had come along at about that time and could cut down heat transfer. To make the Museum of Modern Art chair, we built a drop hammer right in our shop."

Zenith Plastics, the company that made the radar domes, was well known to the Eameses, who had used the company's plastic gas tank linings for making the Japanese doors (*shoji*) in their celebrated house. The company had also molded a chaise longue Eames had designed. Like the domes, the chaise had been made by a slow, costly hand process: woven cloth with fibers embedded in it was immersed in a series of quick-catalyzing resins, laid up by hand and then sandpapered.

Desperate for sample chairs to show at the upcoming Chicago furniture market, Eppinger went out to the Zenith plant, described the sheet metal chairs to Zenith President Milt Brucker and asked what it would cost to make some up to show in Chicago.

Once again, a providential event was about to take place. Zenith Plastics was seeking an entry into the consumer market, and Brucker suggested mass producing the chairs with hydraulic presses. He summoned an engineer, Sol Fingerhut, who said the job could be done with a matched metal mold that would cost about $5,000. (Eames remembers it as finally having cost $20,000.)

Eppinger proposed that Zenith and Herman Miller split the mold costs. "If we do," he added, "what would it cost to make the armchair shells?" Those were the most complicated to fabricate.

The engineer fiddled with a slide rule for a minute. Since pricing was figured entirely in terms of tonnage of resin, it was easy to estimate the cost: $6.25 each, based on an initial run of 10,000.

Eppinger sat down at a typewriter in the plant manager's office and on a yellow second sheet typed out a contract between the two companies. "At this point, Eames knew nothing about it and De Pree knew nothing about it," Eppinger says. "That's the way we could operate then.

"I went back to my room at the Beverly Carlton Hotel, which was where I stayed because Alvin Lustig had worked on the design." (What other company would have a salesman who chose his hotel on the basis of who designed it?) "I called Mr. De Pree and told him what I had done. It didn't take him any time to figure out that 10,000 chairs at $6.25 came to $62,500, and there was just no such thing at Herman Miller. He instructed me to get them to reduce the run to 2,000, which Zenith (later to become Century Plastics) agreed to do. They really were anxious to get into a new

The Design of Herman Miller The Flowering of Design

"Eden" print by Alexander Girard. Photography by Jon Naar.

The Design of Herman Miller 　　　　　The Flowering of Design

Geometric panel designed by Alexander Girard. Photograph by Don Wiechec.

The Design of Herman Miller

The Flowering of Design

market. And that's how the molded fiberglass chair came into being.

"Or rather, that's how it *began.* It came into being through the research that Charles did, largely. His contribution to the company has always gone far beyond design. It was always a contribution in research, in product development, in engineering."

In the case of the plastic chair, product development was plagued by what Eames remembers as "really miserable problems." These ranged from the hazard created by glass particles flying in the air at the plant to the challenge of devising a technique for letting the fibers show through the surface without roughness. With the help of Fingerhut, Brucker, and Irv Green of Zenith, such problems were solved over a nine-month period of intensive work. Even so, each of the early shells was practically handcrafted and the entire surface of each finished shell was gone over with emery cloth.

The emphasis Gilbert Rohde had given to Herman Miller was expressed in furniture that was simple and often neutral in character. Alexander Girard diminished the neutrality with fabric designs that broke the tradition of conservative color use to which all furniture companies, including Herman Miller, were at that time bound.

An architect, Girard began designing fabrics because what he needed was not available.

"We were doing a lot of interior work then," he explains, "and never could find the primary colors we wanted to use; there just were no primary colors available in this field. So we always had them made or dyed or found them in Macy's basement."

The fact that Macy's basement was the chief repository of primary colors indicates the prevailing safety standards for taste in design. "There was a fixed tradition of what was good taste in architecture, furniture, and everything else," Girard says. "In those days a brilliant pink or magenta carried a connotation of double-barreled horror."

Of his contribution to Herman Miller, Girard says: "I see my role—and have always seen my role—with Herman Miller as one of adding to what they have, making things more palatable. One reason for Herman Miller's interest in me — which started with a suggestion Charles made either to George or to one of the De Prees—was that they could never find any appropriate fabrics to put on the furniture or to use for window treatment in showrooms.

"Herman Miller then was the kind of client which we get rarely and which are by far the best. They would stick you with a problem: 'You know about it, you do it.' Then you knock yourself out, because when you have that kind of responsibility you can't blame anyone else if it's no good."

The Design of Herman Miller The Flowering of Design

Action Office open-frame glazing panel is joined to acoustical panel covered with Mexicotton fabric by Girard. Photograph by Don Wiechec.

In 1952, Herman Miller formed a Textile Division, with Girard as director of design. That division produced, in addition to all the company's upholstery fabrics, a full line of casement fabrics and a large selection of Girard prints that were custom printed and cut on individual orders.

The fabrics attracted many customers who wanted to buy small quantities. There was a constant call for just a yard at a time, Girard says, and he and D. J. talked about the possibility of making the fabrics available to people without their having to go through the showroom procedure. The solution seemed to be a textile shop, a sort of ground-floor retail showroom, right on the sidewalk. "Then in the process," Girard says, "we added a lot of other nonsense.... A textile shop sounded awfully dull to me."

The resultant shop was called Textiles and Objects or, familiarly, T & O. The "other nonsense" included a few Herman Miller stools, but consisted mainly of decorative accessories chosen by Girard from various countries.

T & O was a critical, rather than a market, success. Designers and tasteful browsers loved it, and there was at times a fairly brisk trade. But it was brisk in a way that had more to do with retail shop criteria than with a company seeking to make its mark in contract furniture. When, in 1963, the New York showroom moved to Madison Avenue, T & O — which had been just off Madison Avenue — was closed, indicating that the company had come to think of it as a kind of auxiliary showroom, rather than a profit center.

Girard also designed a Herman Miller furniture group, used at L'Etoile, a French restaurant in Manhattan. The restaurant abruptly closed, and the space is now occupied by an airlines ticket center. A couple of the chairs are still there, in red, white, and blue, which happens to work very well for American Airlines.

The contribution of designers to Herman Miller has never been confined to a design contribution. For example, Nelson understood, as the company had not (and *has* not since) always understood, that publicity and advertising must match the design in quality. (Eames took advertising photographs himself, sometimes shooting chairs in the parking lot behind his office, while neighborhood children looked on in fascination.) Nelson persuaded Herman Miller to begin advertising in *Interiors* magazine, insisting on full-page, three-color ads. When D. J. said they couldn't afford that, Nelson advised him to advertise less often.

"If there were sales meetings," Hugh De Pree says, "George and Charles would be there. Also, they were somewhat involved in manufacturing. I doubt that any other company in the industry ever had that kind of close relationship with its designers. And in time we had to get rid of the idea that the designer was God, because we had fallen into the habit of invariably asking, 'What does George think?' or 'What does Charles think?' no matter what the subject was. They used to accuse us of asking them to design us out of situations. I can remember George in particular saying, 'Stop asking us to design you out of this problem. A new product isn't going to solve it.' "

Ironically, design-as-an-instrument-for-dealing-with-situations is pretty close to what many designers today would consider ideal. What many designers in the fifties regarded as ideal was the Nelson-Eames-Girard relationship with their client. Herman Miller people today speak of a "new thrust" that precludes such a relationship. In any case, as Nelson, Eames, Propst, and even the De Prees point out, good as it seemed, it never was ideal.

The Design of Herman Miller

Stock certificate designed by the Eames office was used until Herman Miller went public in 1970.

The Flowering of Design

Color section: Page 65, both factory and logo designed by Nelson; page 66, Nelson storage system; page 67, Nelson sling sofa; page 68, Eames shell chairs; page 69, Eames shell; page 70, Eames lounge chair and ottoman; page 71, Propst's Co/Struc; page 72, Propst's Action Office.

The Design of Herman Miller   The Flowering of Design

The Design of Herman Miller The Flowering of Design

The Design of Herman Miller   The Flowering of Design

The Design of Herman Miller   The Flowering of Design

The Design of Herman Miller The Flowering of Design

69

The Design of Herman Miller　　　　　　The Flowering of Design

The Design of Herman Miller The Flowering of Design

71

The Design of Herman Miller 　　　　The Flowering of Design

The Design of Herman Miller   Branching Out: Propst

It was Charles Eames who insisted (although he didn't necessarily get his way) that the Herman Miller product be "unassailable in the marketplace." Like other companies Herman Miller has a center for materials research and testing, and product engineering. Few manufacturers of any size could survive today without such a research facility for product development and product improvement.

But there is another kind of research operation that bears the Herman Miller name—one calculated to lead the company into new places and to solve problems without any regard for what Herman Miller can or ought to make. This operation, unique in the industry, is the Herman Miller Research Corporation, located in a small research park in Ann Arbor, Michigan. There, in an atmosphere so deeply permeated with quiet efficiency that it looks like a three-dimensional advertisement for Action Office, Robert Propst and his staff work on a staggering range of projects, all of them far afield from traditional Herman Miller activities.

Propst, at this writing, has work in progress on an installation combining Co/Struc and Action Office as a complete facility system for warehousing, transportation, inventory management, technological space and laboratories. For the University of Massachusetts, the Research Corporation recently conducted a dormitory experiment designed to find a basis for making dormitories satisfying enough to keep students from either eschewing or destroying them. At the Southern Methodist University Business School, Propst is also exploring the design of an environment for a new approach to business school education.

Another project, with the Michigan State University College of Agriculture, involves the complete redesign and redirection of an old campus facility to increase both its use and its pedagogical effectiveness.

"Michigan State came to us with a problem that was classic in its zero potential," Propst says. "They told us that there was no budget, that professors were not going to change, that the buildings were not going to change, and that there was no accountability — you couldn't prove whether anything was helping or hurting." The Herman Miller Research proposal was approved and budgeted, however; the building was converted; and researchers from both Michigan State and Herman Miller have tested the facility's effectiveness with encouraging results.

The space conversion has taken the form of a "Lecture-Lab Center for Responsive Educational Services," designed to make instructional materials accessible to students at all times. One of the key ingredients in the new facility is a "resource service store," which supplies slide and tape programs and equipment, offers a tape duplication service for students who want to buy their own tapes, and includes a supplementary reference library, a service desk, and a lounge and coffee bar. Students are told, "The 'store' is in the business of putting programs, tools, and information at your disposal. If something doesn't work, the store will fix or replace it." (And the experiment has now attracted faculty members impressed by how effectively the place works. So perhaps some of the professors *are* changing.)

Other Research Corporation projects range even further afield, or seem to. For Kimberly-Clark, they prepared a study of the ramifications of single-use products—a matter properly of concern to the manufacturers of Kleenex. At the other extreme from mass production, they have spent months redesigning and equipping an office-van for a quadriplegic lawyer with a clientele of handicapped people in New York City.

The range reflects Propst's diverse interests and his conviction that "diversity keeps the innovation process healthy." A case in point is the Propst Timber Harvester, a machine that enables one man to de-root, de-limb, top, and cut four trees a minute! The concept behind the machine is vertical harvesting, which makes tree-felling unnecessary, at spectacular savings of time and space.

The timber harvester operator drives a vehicle invented and designed by Propst and his associates. As the tree is sheared from its root, it is clasped against a toothed lift chain. The tree is then raised, placed at the mouth of a cut-off shear, and automatically lowered, upright, while six-foot lengths are cut off the bottom and kicked into a conveyer. At the same time, the limbs are being trimmed from the log. The first machines have been sold to the pulp and paper companies that were the chief supporters of the research.

Sliding sharply in scale from the timber harvester is HMRC's study of the "proximate environment"—the collection of small objects that workers personally handle: paper clips, tape cassettes, wastebaskets, pens, pencils and markers, staplers, stamps, desk calculators, in and out boxes, briefcases, etc. Propst, with associate Bill Stumpf, is developing a complete set of complementary proximate environment components.

Propst sees the proximate environment project as a direct extension of Action Office and Co/Struc, with such a large collection of products that "it is relatively unimportant whether people like or dislike individual products. In the end the major general usefulness just becomes abundantly apparent, representing an entirely different world from the one in which you try to seize people with 'Look at the dandy new gadget.'"

Although John De Pree is the only one of D J.'s three sons not in Herman Miller Inc., he played an indirect part in Robert Propst's

The Design of Herman Miller Branching Out: Propst

Propst Timber Harvester enables one man to de-root, de-limb, top, and cut four trees a minute.

emergence as a Herman Miller resource. Now chairman of the department of mathematics at New Mexico State University, John was in graduate school at the University of Colorado in the midfifties. While visiting him there, D. J. heard of Propst and called on him.

Propst at that time was sculpting, sketching, and inventing. He had begun a successful architectural sculpture business and had developed a series of contracts for sponsored innovative activities with companies in the lumber, aviation, and precast concrete industries.

Herman Miller was not a new name to Propst (he had actually gone to Zeeland a couple of years before to show his fishbone connector — an ingenious device for quickly joining knock-down furniture components), but he found it hard to relate the company to any of his current interests. D. J. found it easy, however, and called Hugh from Boulder to insist that they sign Propst up.

The initial arrangement gave Propst a retainer to spend two-fifths of his time working on company projects on a fee basis. His Herman Miller–sponsored research during this period included studies of human factors in work stations, the development of a litter for burn victims, and a mechanical and automatic bed-chair for quadriplegics.

That arrangement continued until 1960, when the Herman Miller Research Corporation was formed, primarily as a good way of using Bob Propst. It is located in Ann Arbor to take advantage of University of Michigan research facilities, but also because a certain distance from the parent company is desirable to Propst, a man described by himself and others as cherishing a bristly independence.

At its inception, the Research Corporation began developing the ideas that became Action Office. Although Propst's assignment was to explore problems for which "a product not necessarily furniture" might be the solution, the first general problem he focused on was the office; and the basic product, though not the only one, was furniture.

The original Action Office (now called Action Office 1) was a union of Propst's ideas and development and Nelson's design details. It received wide and favorable national publicity, but did not sell well. Hugh De Pree now feels that it did not deserve to: "Action Office 1 was poorly made, it wasn't really a system, and it was extremely high priced to boot."

Propst is convinced that the present Action Office (Action Office 2) would be greatly improved if it were better used and that optimal use depends upon the company's getting more information to the user.

"Right now we're telling the user about 10 percent of what we could be telling him," Propst says. "Information is not just something for the advertising people to play around with. Their objectives and sales objectives are a lot different from the kind of *information product* I'm talking about. They're like people picking over the Thanksgiving Day turkey: they take a little of this and a little of that.

"Information is at least 50 percent of the system product — maybe more — and what I'm talking about is one of the most important areas of product development — information on different ways of living in an institutional context. We should be developing a whole new system of reinforcing components: books, publications, audio-visual materials, conferences." Some of these items the Research Corporation has already produced, most recently *The Action Office Acoustic Handbook* by Propst and Michael Wodka.

One of the functions of the Research Corporation is to gain access to levels of management that neither a designer nor a furniture company could reach. If you come on as a designer, Propst points out, management wants you to talk to their architect or their art department. "The design image itself keeps you from having access to the right people, and of course no one wants to talk to a furniture company about information handling. But a demonstrably bona fide research corporation is something else. For example, no one in the agricultural industry had ever heard of us. But we had an authentic strategy for getting involved in the problem. We didn't invent or design a damned thing until we had a complete profile of what needed to be done.

"A lot of interesting problems I see are supposed to be handled by industries that aren't ready to take them on. Take the timber harvester, for example. We didn't go to the machine industry; we went to the pulp industry. They were the ones who had the problem, they were the ones who needed the solution, and they were the ones who were prepared to give us support in a partnership relationship. They had a lot of the information we needed. They taught us what we needed to know about what the machine needed to do. If we'd gone to a manufacturer with a position in the market, they'd want something they could fasten on the front end of something they already have in the line."

Robert Propst already had a good patent on the vertical harvesting principle, and his brother Howard spent six months in the South developing criteria for the timber harvester. The Propsts studied the scale of trees, terrain variations, mill procedures, marketing profiles, labor rates, the varying abilities of people in the woods, maintenance and repair patterns, weather, flotation. *Then* they proposed the first prototype.

They were promised support for testing and evaluation if they could deliver the prototype, which they did in six months. It would have taken two years conventionally, according to Propst. After the de-bugging and field-testing program, the Propsts proposed the next step: a production prototype. That took eight months. "We designed the vehicle from

The Design of Herman Miller

Branching Out: Propst

Action Office components can be arranged in a variety of configurations, including both open plan and private spaces.

The Design of Herman Miller Branching Out: Propst

Action Office accessories include magnetic belt tray, foot rail, tray stand holder, reader stand, EDP reader stand, lockable roll top.

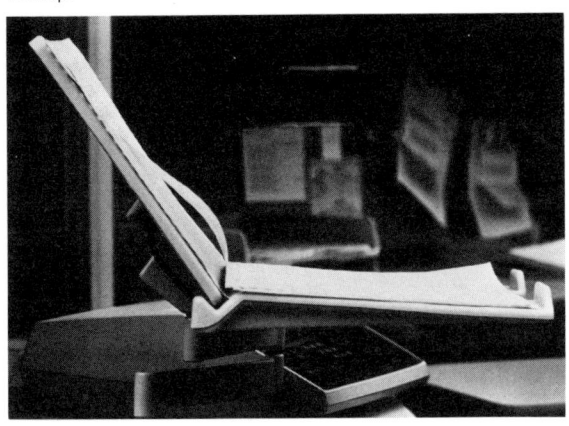

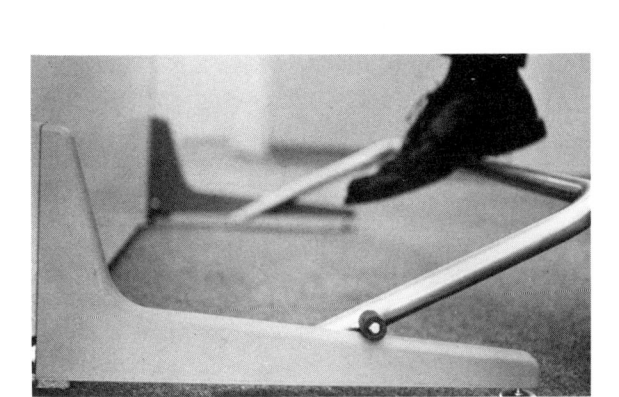

scratch!" Propst says. "If an equipment manufacturer had taken on something like this, it would have taken years and well over a million bucks. And they wouldn't have had the motivation to design a vehicle from scratch. In fact, they would have had the motivation *not* to design a vehicle from scratch."

The Research Corporation's diversity reflects Bob Propst's conviction that an organization like his can't put all its eggs in one basket. If it did, it could never afford to lay one—a luxury of risk essential to creative action. Neither can it afford to be at the mercy of circumstantial change.

"Here's why problem-solving *systems* interest me so much," Propst says. "Depending on what's going on in hospital at any given time, the big issue of the day may be sterilization or sanitization. Now if a product like Co/Struc were to take sanitization as its entire basis, somebody could develop a spray that would knock the whole concern down. We have to consider the surrounding issues: patient care, hospital logistics, personnel problems, communication problems, food."

The alacrity with which Herman Miller Inc. moved into systems was both remarkable and practical. "They're very good at being schizophrenic and multiphilosophied," Propst says. "They could accept somebody's coming along with a new thing counter to what they already had. Also they saw almost at once that they would have nothing if they didn't have the collection of reinforcing solutions—which is pretty much what a system really is.

"The premise for both Action Office and Co/Struc was the total package. You either had X number of things or you didn't have anything. Herman Miller was able to accept that premise, but the classic organizational reaction would be, 'it's dangerous to try all those products at once. Let's start with one or two of them and build up.'

"Herman Miller put millions into working on problems, which is darned unusual for a company their size, and they didn't go to a famous furniture designer. They put all their activities into the hands of a pretty unknown person out of nowhere."

One goal of the Research Corporation is to keep the parent company constantly off-center, far enough ahead to have solutions by the time they are marketable. The relationship between the two companies is a project relationship, depending on Propst's proposing interesting things for Herman Miller Inc. to do.

"Unfortunately," he says, "we propose more things than they *can* do, but I think the Strategy and Development Division that Max heads up will give us a new and healthier emphasis."

The purpose of Max De Pree's division is to come up with a new program every three to

The Design of Herman Miller Branching Out: Propst

Co/Struc laboratory installation.

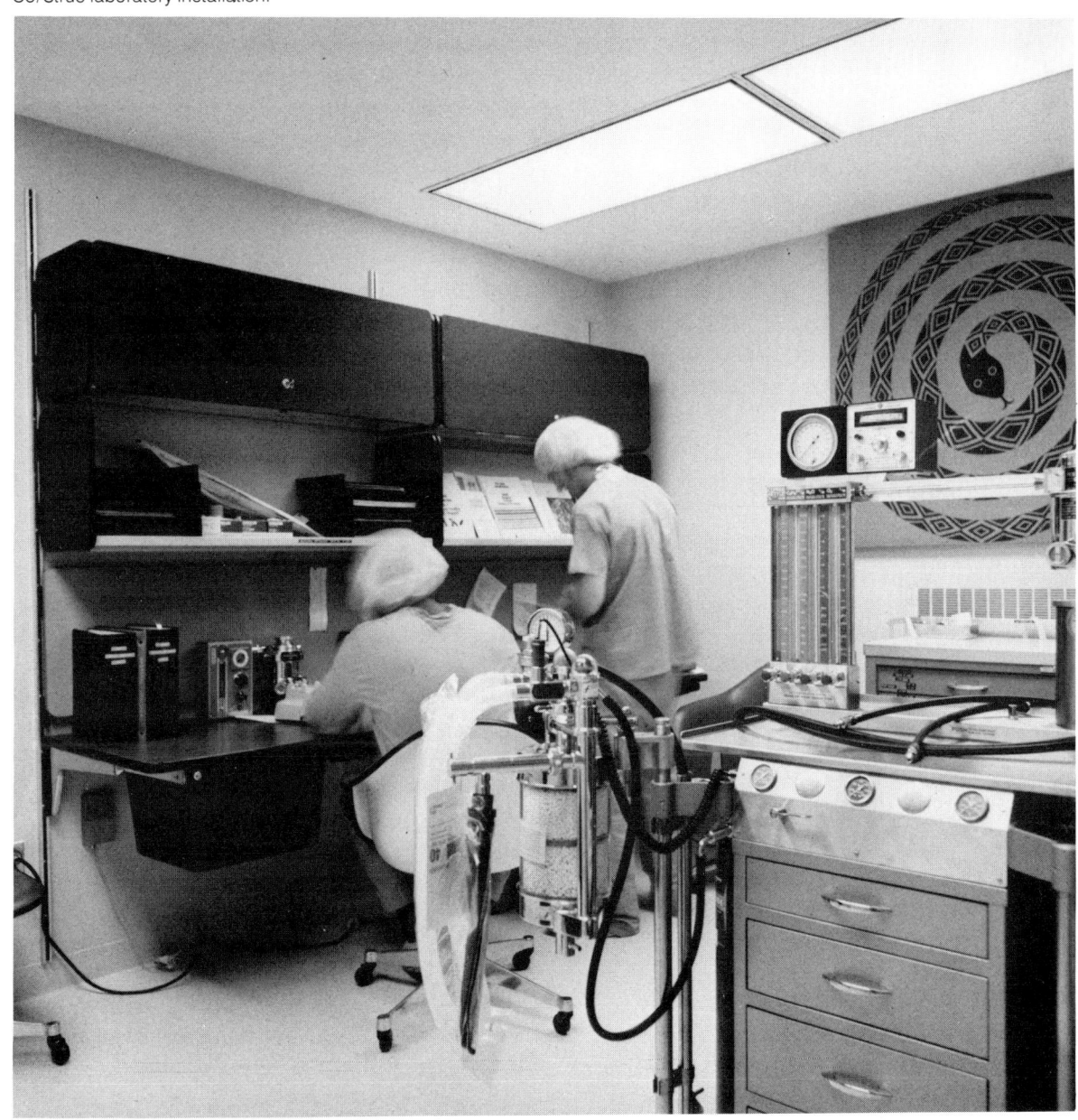

five years. "There is a certain kind of climate required in order to get good ideas," Max says, "a climate of receptivity—a climate in which implementation can occur."

According to Propst, that climate is there already, although the weather is variable. "One of Herman Miller's most unusual decisions was to let things happen here no matter what they turned out to be. Not many people in the company initially wanted to enter the spheres we were leading them into, but Hugh De Pree made that decision."

It was a practical decision and was kept practical by support from chief financial officer Vern Poest. "For a creative group to survive as long as ours has," Propst says, "you have to have financial discipline. Working with Vern Poest gave us insights into financial reporting and program control that were a big advantage. It also gave us access to Herman Miller's internal financial perspective, so we knew what they could and couldn't do.

"Now they have some of their best talent expanding ours; like having Joe Schwartz [vice-president, Health/Science Group] head up the health-care program. Schwartz realizes that the systems are only as important as the information about how to use them correctly, and he was the first to see that the ordinary efforts were inadequate. Glenn Walters really saw a critical difference in what was needed and gave Joe Schwartz the freedom and authority to do something highly innovative in sales and marketing—the Action Office seminar program. We never would have got to those people through the dealers or our own salesmen. Schwartz didn't overstate, he didn't say dumb things about what the system could do, he didn't let it get driven into simplistic terms, which is what's happening in the open-planning market right now. His contribution at that point was essential."

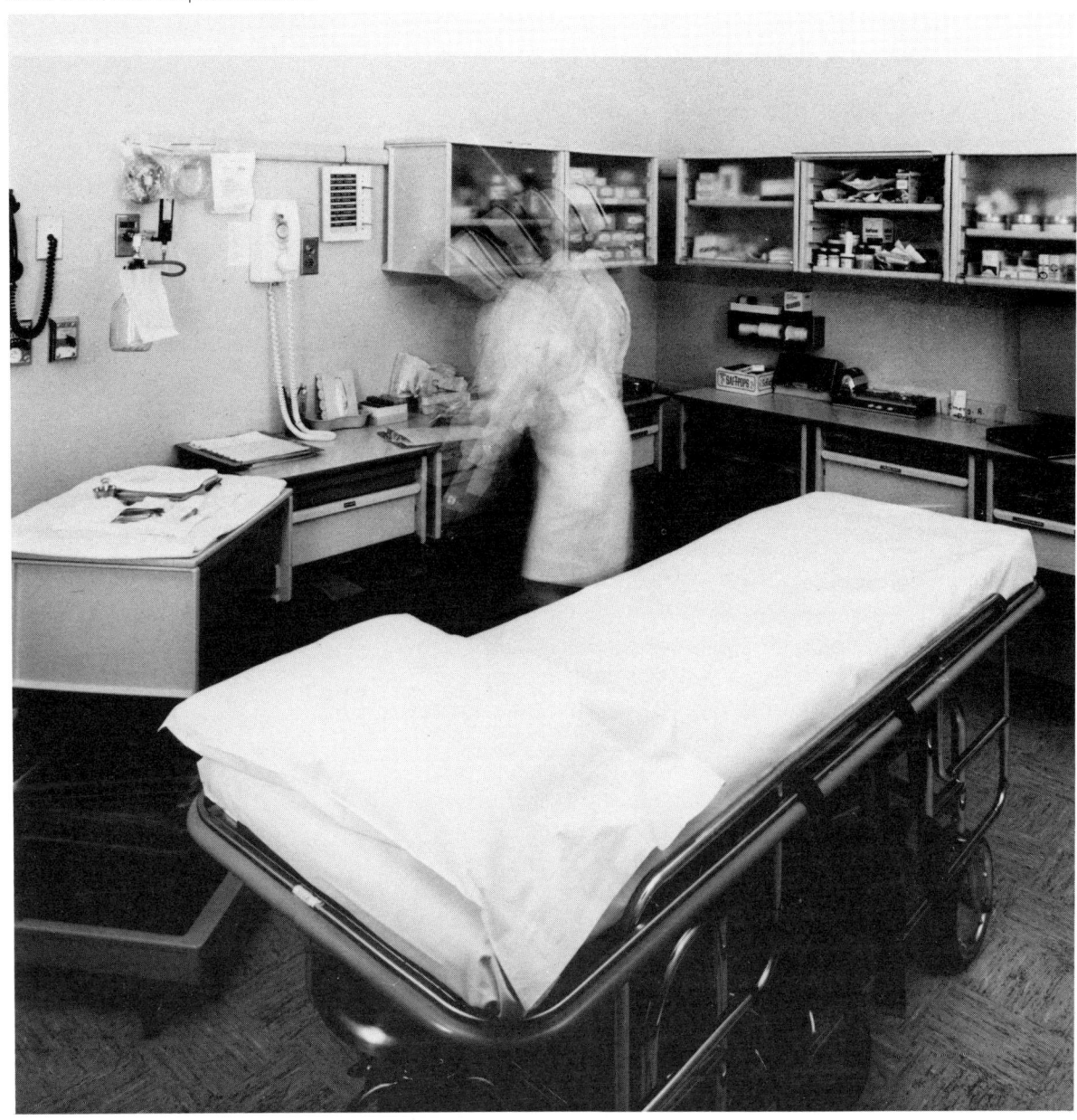

The Design of Herman Miller Branching Out: Propst

Nurse in Co/Struc hospital installation.

My Life in an Action Office

Although Action Office accounts for the largest share of Herman Miller's volume, it probably has less "visibility" than many other items in the line. It is not encountered in homes, or in airport lobbies and other public spaces, and is not the stuff of which dreams or magazine photographer's backgrounds are made.

The renown that certain of Charles Eames's designs have achieved through their ubiquity has been heightened by their imitators. This is not true of Action Office, although it may be the most widely imitated of the Herman Miller line. Because one of the features of the system is a certain lack of visual distinction, AO's functional distinction may get lost in the sea of copies. As with other widely imitated inventions, the surface aspects of Action Office are easiest to reproduce. The system is designed more as a process than as product. The process is harder to describe, sell, or copy; yet it, rather than the product, is the basis for the system's success.

Not that the product is easy to copy. A couple of years ago I met with designers in a large corporation that manufacturers a competitive open-planning furniture line. Because it was a shirt-sleeves meeting, I hung up my jacket. It fell down. I hung it up again. It fell down again.

"How comes it keeps falling down?" I asked.

"I know why," one of the designers replied. "The coat hook is the only part of this entire system that we didn't rip off from Herman Miller."

"Organizations that have used Action Office well," Propst says, "have experienced evolutionary changes in which the system is a sensitive part of the process, a malleable place that adjusts to management needs." But while Action Office made its reputation for its flexibility in large, complicated installations, I can best describe it as applied to a deliberately quick and easy setup for a tiny operation: my own. This book in fact is being written in an environment created specifically for this book to be written in. When the job is done, the components can be reassembled in minutes into another kind of environment for another kind of job.

Here is how it happened. One day I was visiting the Herman Miller New York showroom with a friend who was seeing it for the first time. Impressed with the ambience, he said, "If I were writing a book about this company, I'd do it right here."

"In the *showroom?*"

"Sure," he said.

"It's a funny idea," I said without laughing.

On second thought it wasn't so funny. The Action Office system was bound to figure in this book. So why not do the work in an Action

The Design of Herman Miller My Life in an Action Office

Office to see how the system works? Furthermore, in the New York headquarters, I would be surrounded by products, systems, and people associated with the company.

But did I *want* to be surrounded by a lot of people? No. Wasn't it hard enough to get work done anyway? Yes. Still, this was one of the myriad problems Action Office was supposed to address, and it seemed worth checking out. Also, as my friend had observed, the showroom was nicer than where I usually hang out.

"Here?" showroom manager John Buglisi asked, when I broached the subject.

"Sure," I said.

"It's a funny idea," he said without laughing.

Providentially (in line with a concept treated elsewhere) a salesman had just left the company, and I moved into his office or — as Propst prefers to call it — his "work station."

There was a gross violation of Propstian theory in my misusing the system by trying to perform one kind of work in an environment set up for another kind. Propst was right about that, too, as I discovered the first day. I had the wrong components in the wrong configuration. Clearly what I needed was an office designed on the basis of an analysis of the task and my needs in performing it. Tom Newhouse, a designer in the company's Design and Development group, asked me to set it all down, and I sent him the following memo.

"This is to be a work station designed for a temporary task—namely, the research and preparation of a small book about Herman Miller. There are two people working on this project—a writer and a research assistant. (Neither of them uses the facility full time.)

"The in-office part of the work consists essentially of reading and handling masses of material (much of it oversized), writing up notes and rough drafts, and producing final manuscripts. Some of the material is on tape cassettes and will be transcribed in the office.

"A fair amount of telephoning is required.

"Privacy is essential. At the same time it is useful to interact frequently with the people in the Herman Miller showroom.

"We need ample surface space for spreading out paper. This surface should be a stand-up height, and wide enough to permit two people to examine the same stuff at the same time.

"Much of the first draft will be dictated, then typed. But some will be rough-written first, then retyped. So we need provision for comfortable person-to-person dictation, and also a typewriter within easy reach of the desk surface.

"Because the material is confidential, a lockable file bin is required.

"For layout and organization, at least two tackboard modules are needed."

As a writer on design I have from time to time railed against the unplanned environment; yet my own work had taken place exclusively in a series of what Propst calls environmental accidents. Now, on a very small scale, I was telling a designer my needs in the way that a client for a house tells an architect his or hers. What was strange about the situation was its rarity; for *all* offices should be approached this way.

I flooded Tom Newhouse with some extra considerations regarding personal habits. I pace while dictating, make notes while on the phone, write far more than I can possibly use, tend to misplace things, am easily seduced into distracting conversations. I spread paper on every available surface, including the floor, and since I have a bad back, the only way to work with material on the floor is to get down on the floor with it. I am diverted by ambient noise, but in this instance was ambivalent about it — I wanted to eavesdrop. As my research assistant, Mary Cunniff, kept saying, everything we overheard was true grist for our mill.

At first, that mill ground exceeding slow. Newhouse responded quickly with the sketch on the opposite page, but it took a while to locate the basic components — I never got them all — and find someone who knew how to put them all together and could spare the time to do it. At last, Larry Pond, a designer in Design Resource Services, set it up with the assistance of maintenance man Tom Hughie.

We have been using the system sporadically and learning from it for several months. Here are a few things I learned (none of which was news to Bob Propst).

1. *The effectiveness of the system depends upon its correct use, which in turn depends on learning how to use it.* In our haste, Mary and I didn't spend enough time finding out what it was all about. This was not catastrophic for us, but it was troublesome enough to make clear that it could be catastrophic in a larger and more complicated installation. "You can make a really terrible place out of a system like this," Propst says, "because its permissiveness can have negative effects as well as positive ones. There are Action Office installations that are miserably designed and applied."

But there are of course many open-planning installations — including AO imitations — that are much more miserably designed and applied. Systems that are superficially like AO often are not as "forgiving," to use Propst's term for his system's resilience in letting the user correct mistakes.

The Design of Herman Miller My Life in an Action Office

Writer's work station.

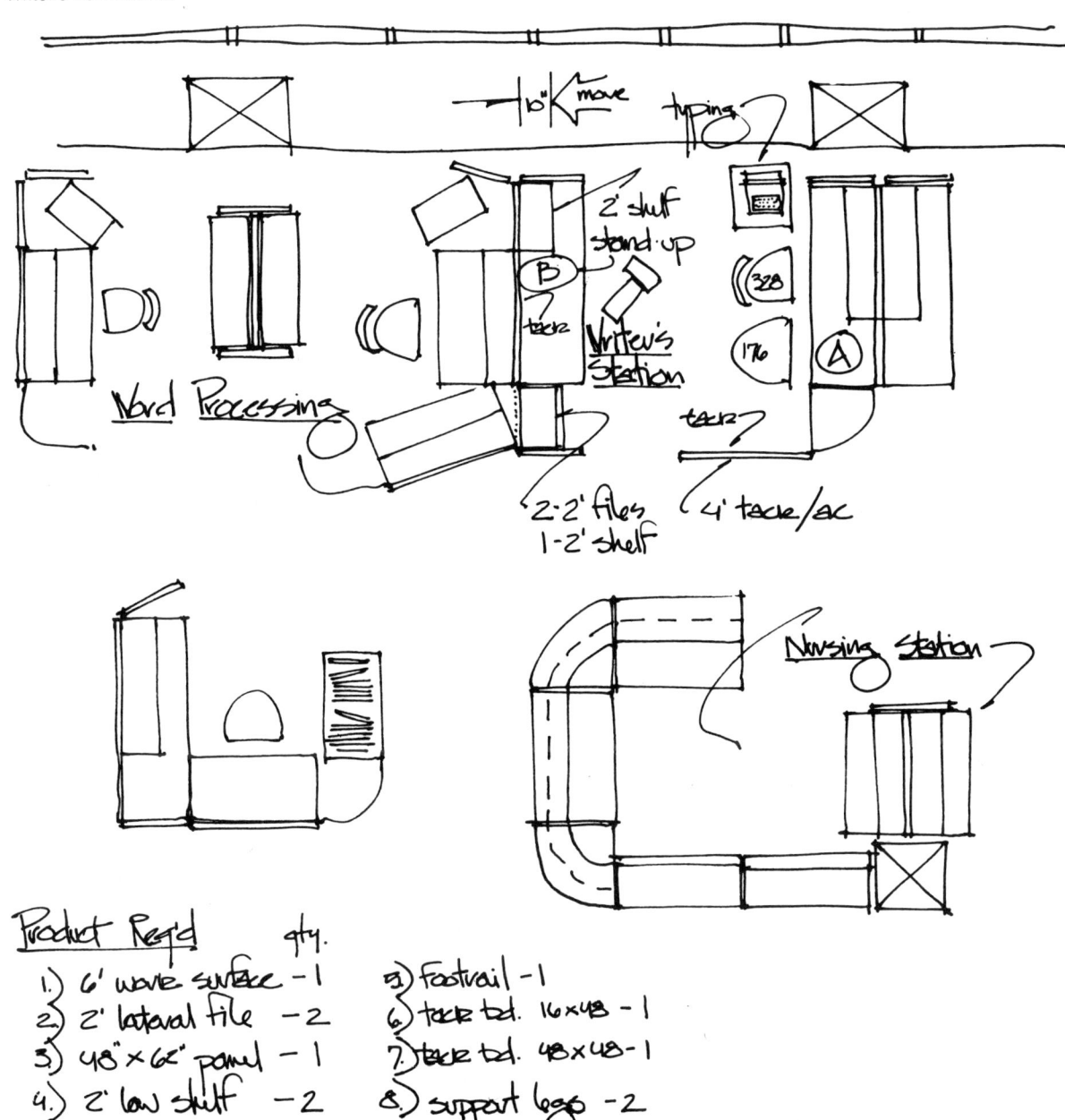

Product Req'd qty.
1.) 6' wave surface – 1
2.) 2' lateral file – 2
3.) 48" x 62" panel – 1
4.) 2' low shelf – 2
5.) Footrail – 1
6.) tack bd. 16x48 – 1
7.) tack bd. 48x48 – 1
8.) support legs – 2

The Design of Herman Miller My Life in an Action Office

Action Office ambiance varies with the use to which the system is put and the information and sensitivity with which it is installed. The system, in Propst's terms, "forgives" mistakes.

The Design of Herman Miller   My Life in an Action Office

Action Office "Perch" makes it possible to sit, or perch, at stand-up desk.

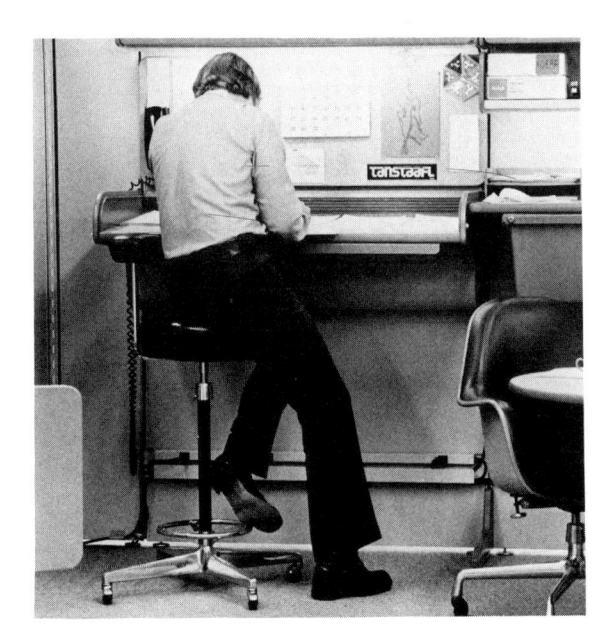

2. *The effectiveness of the system depends on the right combination of components.* I knew that I needed a stand-up desk; I did not know that I needed a stand-up desk with a closable top. Without that feature, all of the papers spread out during the day had to be put away at the end of the day and resurrected the next time I needed them, thus reinforcing my own tendency toward discontinuity. Another, less important, omission was the foot rail, which I wanted partly for comfort and partly as a nostalgic reminder of a misspent youth.

To be sure, I probably could have gotten these items, but having them was less important to me than figuring out why they were needed. To a genuine customer, however, having them would be essential, which is why Herman Miller places so much emphasis on accurate identification of user needs.

3. *A system designed to encourage desirable habits requires that you meet it halfway in consciously developing such habits.* Propst puts a great deal of emphasis on information display and upon the exploitation of vertical surfaces, such as shelves and tackboards. I obediently pinned up an assortment of self-directed reminders and injunctions. But at first they remained there for days without my even noticing them, because I was not accustomed to looking at the wall for instructions. The effect was precisely that of Poe's purloined letter: the best place to hide something is in plain view. Mary often eschewed the display principle and hid things in drawers, with what Propst calls "disastrous squirreling-away-and-die consequences to information."

Not only did the work station have to be tuned like a musical instrument, but only when we learned to play it did we get the notes we wanted. It is always satisfying to discover that a design anticipates your needs. Action Office does this largely through its wealth of support details: an array of such accessories as pivot-arm reading stands, cassette trays, chalkboards, vinyl folders and binders, and even spine labels that are part of the system. These are often very precise tools for keeping within reach the things you need, for keeping out of the way the things you don't need, and for quickly seeing which is which.

4. *Every system has to take into account the larger system around it.* If you look at Tom Newhouse's sketch, you will see that my office was adjacent to a model "word-processing office" to the north. What the sketch does not show is that on the other side we were adjacent to the work station of Jack Eiel, a regional sales manager of Health/Science, and it was hard to keep from hearing Eiel's telephone conversations. Notice too that my office is across from a "nursing station." Like the word-processing station, this is an uninhabited demonstration unit. But it turned out to be an almost irresistible space for stand-up conversations between salesmen and customers.

The Design of Herman Miller My Life in an Action Office

At first I couldn't understand the insensitivity of people who would hold 30-minute conversations only a few feet from where I was trying to think. But of course a furniture showroom is not normally a place where concentrated work is done. *We* were the interlopers.

The solutions are designed into the system: acoustical paneling, white sound generators, and even an easily set up, movable "super room" — a private room with its own lighting and ventilation system.

5. *No system is magic.* "Design," George Nelson once wrote, "cannot transform a dark brown little life into a large, brightly colored one." Well, I hadn't expected Action Office design to do *that,* but I had hoped it would transform my disorganized life into an orderly one. It hasn't yet, but it has gone further in that direction than any other equipment I have ever used, and could go further if I let it.

Action Office "Perch" makes it possible to sit, or perch, at stand-up desk.

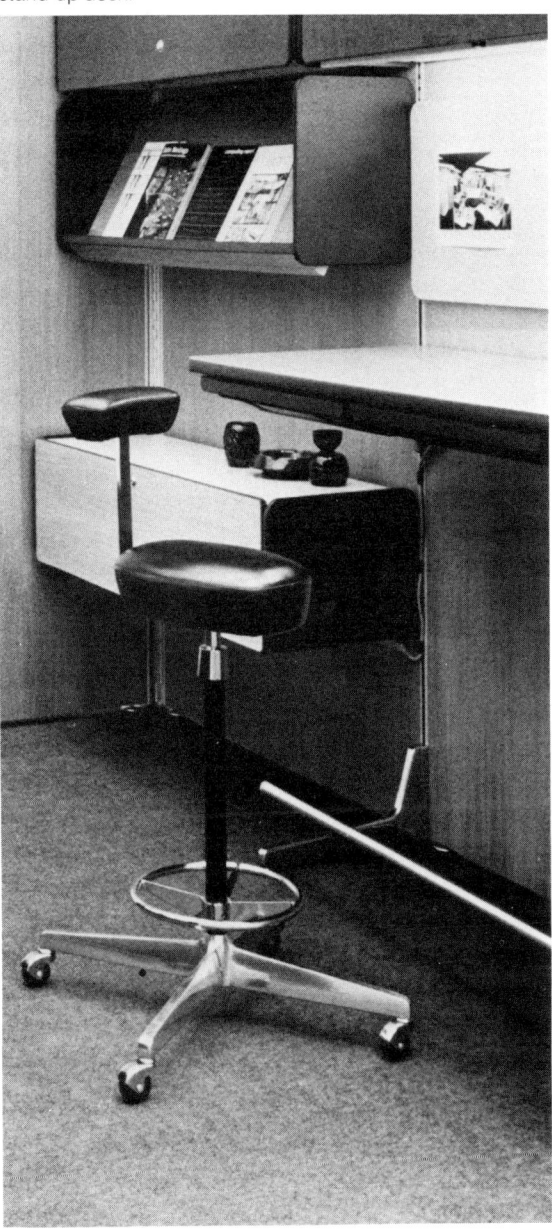

The Design of Herman Miller

Redesigning the Family Tree

Just as you can't talk for long about Herman Miller past apart from the designers, you can't talk about Herman Miller present and future without using them as a reference point. Glenn Walters, executive vice-president of the Office/Institutional Division, sees the future as characterized by marketing emphasis, but adds, "In my opinion the marketing emphasis in this company really began with George Nelson.

"In other words, marketing was always important at Herman Miller, but the means by which we implement it has changed. We're moving out of the genius designer phase of the business, but one reason that phase was so successful is that, as it happened, the designers of the past were superb marketing people.

"That phase seems to have run roughly in ten-year cycles. Nelson was the guiding genius from the midforties to the midfifties, Eames from the midfifties to the midsixties, and Propst from the midsixties to the present. That, of course, is an oversimplification. The genius of all three is reflected in the line still, and the impact of each of them was felt beyond three decades. But with each decade the firm took on new characteristics. The genius of Eames and Propst is obviously a continuing influence on what the company does, but not to the same degree as in the past.

"What we're doing now involves far more people and more discipline in the feedback process — engineering, cost, price strata market size, distribution," Walters says.

Hugh De Pree adds:

"The extent of their impact on the business began to change in the late fifties. Our needs were becoming a little different — we were growing, for one thing. We were getting into the institutional and contract business, not so much because George and Charles thought that was what we ought to do, but because some of our salesmen began to see that market as the right place for what George and Charles had designed.

"So other people started to have comparatively more influence on the business. At the same time, I think, George and Charles were changing in their own interests, in the amount of time they wanted to allocate to Herman Miller.

"The turning point really came with Action Office. The systems process was different from the piece goods process, although we didn't know it at the time. When Propst came along with his conception, we did what we had been doing right along. We said, 'Here are the ideas. Now, George Nelson, you design the product.' We were surprised that it didn't work; but it didn't, and George could see that it didn't."

Actually, Nelson and Propst had different ideas about the product. Nelson saw it as a

The Design of Herman Miller

Redesigning the Family Tree

number of massively molded parts, while Propst envisioned a highly tooled series of smaller parts that would fit together in a large variety of ways. Hugh De Pree recalls the event that moved him to break the stalemate:

"Propst worked on it his way, and we thought about the problem as we always had. In other words we were thinking, 'Okay, Propst, you're the designer. You go ahead and design all this.' And Propst was making headway, but nothing was happening to move the product through the company.

"Just about that time I attended a seminar in Chicago on office landscaping, and I came away shaken to my boots. There were other people talking about the same thing we had been talking about! I concluded we had to get it on the market, so we took the stuff away from Bob Propst and said, 'This is no longer entirely your responsibility.' I think that was the first time we recognized that some other people might have input into all this. It was also the first time the company was determined to take steps not to be knocked off. There was another first, too: the first time cost goals and price goals became design criteria."

In October, De Pree wrote a short memo to Glenn Walters, appointing him chairman of a committee to get Action Office 2 on the market by June and authorizing him to "do anything necessary except sell the company."

Walters didn't sell the company, and his committee, at one time numbering as many as 50 people, did get the product out for the June market. One of the committee members was Joe Schwartz, the former New York sales manager, who in 1967 had been transferred to Zeeland as marketing manager. Walters, Blaich, and others saw that the innovative concept required an equally innovative way to sell it.

Schwartz agreed, on the basis of his experience in trying to sell Action Office 1 to the New York market in 1964. "It was new, high-priced, hard to ship," he says. "And we hadn't an inkling of how to sell it. Herman Miller's business up to that time had been to improve the esthetic through an art form called furniture."

Or so it may have looked. In fact, the concern was rarely just esthetic. "From the first," Charles Eames says, "I viewed what Propst was doing as an extension of what we were trying to do."

For Action Office 2, Schwartz devised a sales instrument that, in the words of Bob Propst, "was the most critical thing that happened in respect to getting to the people we wanted to reach."

Bob Blaich puts it this way: "What made Action Office 2 fly was the recognition that the architect and the dealer didn't have the problem, the customer had the problem."

That parallels the insight D. J. De Pree had in the early thirties: "... I was learning that we had to get closer to the ultimate user."

The solution Schwartz came up with was a series of seminars unique in two respects. They were unlike the run of company-sponsored seminars in their substance — they contained genuine information rather than sales propaganda. But the truly singular distinction lay in the people to whom they were directed, namely the end users.

"Herman Miller had no expertise in systems like this," Schwartz says. "What were we supposed to do with it? There was no known market for panel-hung accessories. If the salesman couldn't sell concepts, then the dealers certainly couldn't."

Schwartz acted on the hunch that if the customer understood the concept, he would want it, and that the concept was so far from Herman Miller's direct experience—or anyone else's — that there was no use in just having the salesmen understand it. In fact, salesmen were not even allowed to attend the first seminars, although later they were let in a few at a time. Seats at the early seminars were at such a premium that Schwartz even refused to admit D. J. De Pree to one of them, arguing, "You don't buy anything, D. J."

"Glenn threw the marketing problem to Joe in much the same blanket way that I had thrown the project to him," Hugh De Pree says. "In the good old days that wouldn't have happened. The whole idea of setting up an educational center in a really dirty, bankrupt Grand Rapids supermarket and going directly to business people before training our own dealers was Joe's work."

(Schwartz's victory was not total: he lost the battle over the name. "Action Office 2" was chosen despite his strong objection that "it's like naming a car Edsel 2.")

The seminar concept itself is regarded as Schwartz's major contribution to the success of AO 2, but I doubt that anyone else could have brought the idea to fruition. His leadership of the seminars was a series of spectacular performances. Long before "Sesame Street" used television commercial techniques to package elementary school lessons, Joe Schwartz was using the zestful rhythms of an Atlantic City boardwalk pitchman to talk about office planning. Propst and Schwartz perfectly fit the Biblical mode of paraclete and exegete.

The same general strategy is being applied to the company's health-care system, Co/Struc, which presents even greater problems in manufacturing and selling than Action Office did. Herman Miller has made its reputation on design innovation. Co/Struc represents an attempt to extend the reputation through marketing and production innovation. It is, accord-

The Design of Herman Miller Redesigning the Family Tree

Ergon chairs were designed by William Stumpf after long and deep research into ergonomics, or human factors, following tradition of Nelson chair on page 41.

ing to Schwartz, "the first Herman Miller project ever focused on a particular market," although others dispute this, citing, for example, the educational market.

Of course, in retrospect, Herman Miller made what looks like a decisive shift from a residential market to an institutional market. One consultant claims, however, "They never really knew when they were doing it." But at least they knew once they had done it. "If it can't be sold to an airport we don't make it," a sales manager used to tell his staff. The company now intends to be in the residential market, and probably would be even if it didn't intend to; many items obviously work as well in either category.

"When I designed textiles for Herman Miller," Alexander Girard says, "people kept asking, 'What are these for?' I've never made any particular dividing line between residential and office. What are Eames chairs for? You can use them where you want."

Why should a company that had developed, at great cost, strategies for selling residential and office furniture decide to launch its new marketing effort in an alien field such as health care?

"How did we get into the hospital business?" Schwartz asks. "That's easy. Bob Propst slipped his disc. This is a providential company, haven't you heard?"

In point of fact, Propst had been interested in hospitals long before he joined Herman Miller, and the Co/Struc system was developed at the same time Action Office was under development. The marketing plan under way now is a move from hospital furnishings to laboratory furnishings.

Co/Struc is a team effort; after the development of Action Office 2 and a mechanism for selling it, the Glenn Walters committee procedure became a model for future operations. "Design needs the support and protection of other skills and other competence," Walters says. "The present approach really just implements an old recommendation of George Nelson's. 'Everybody knocks us off,' he said, 'so why don't we knock ourselves off?' We used to kid ourselves by thinking that there is no existing reference point. In other words, if there are no other plastic chairs, then we have the market. But with Action Office we have to face a world of people who are satisfied with conventional equipment. We have to satisfy the same people at the same prices."

That argument is expanded by Steven Snoey, executive vice-president of international operations. Like Glenn Walters, who heads the domestic operation, Snoey reports directly to Hugh De Pree.

"Internationally," Snoey says, "we're moving from an era of contractual relationships with licensees to an era of increased corporate responsibility, in the form of either majority control or wholly owned subsidiaries.

"No question about it — we became international through the collection, because of names like Eames, Nelson, Girard. But the collection in itself doesn't provide the balance needed for international success. To achieve that balance in the market we need the interaction of all disciplines, a diverse management team focused on the market. Going public in 1970 meant accountability; it demanded that we become profitable enough to support growth from within. Long before going public we made a commitment to change the balance of the board, and to limit the number of De Prees holding corporate office, in line with the need for more openness to outside influences."

Such changes appear to be inevitable. Milly Teperman, Herman Miller's Brazilian licensee, thinks the times require them. So does Nora Dozeman, who came to work for Herman Miller in 1936 as a sewer, the only woman in the plant. She is still a sewer, still likes it, and is reconciled to the fact that she no longer cuts and sews an entire chair herself. For that matter, the president can no longer go through the plant every day to greet each employee, as D. J. De Pree did. The expanding scale of operations is responsible for new departures.

Yet some things that look like new departures have precedents—or at least false starts—in company history. In the late sixties a particularly trim line of seating was designed by the Nelson office, based on detailed human factors studies done at the University of Tokyo. Partly because of technological obstacles, the line was never produced as designed. But the Ergon chair, designed by Bill Stumpf and introduced in 1976, was developed in that tradition, after Stumpf's probing investigation of what medical researchers had learned. This chair may go further than any other yet produced toward supporting the body in a way that takes anatomical structure into account. Thus it is not only comfortable, which any soft chair can be for a time, but supportive in a way calculated to diminish fatigue and prevent back problems.

Just as Jimmy Eppinger keeps emphasizing that what Herman Miller did in the old days was unplanned and, therefore, all the more startling, Hugh De Pree keeps emphasizing that what Herman Miller does now is pretty close to normal business practice, and *therefore* all the more startling. He cites the group of Ergon chairs designed by Bill Stumpf. The chairs were assigned to Stumpf, who produced some initial ideas, then worked with salespeople, marketing people, and engineers. One of their first findings was that the initial design did not permit the chair to be introduced at a price level that had an opening for it, so the product was redesigned accordingly.

The Design of Herman Miller Redesigning the Family Tree

The Design of Herman Miller Redesigning the Family Tree

1910 work force of the Michigan Star Furniture Company (later to become Herman Miller Inc.) supports their local ball club. Companywide festivities continue, with contemporary design support such as the highly coveted picnic posters by Stephen Frykholm.

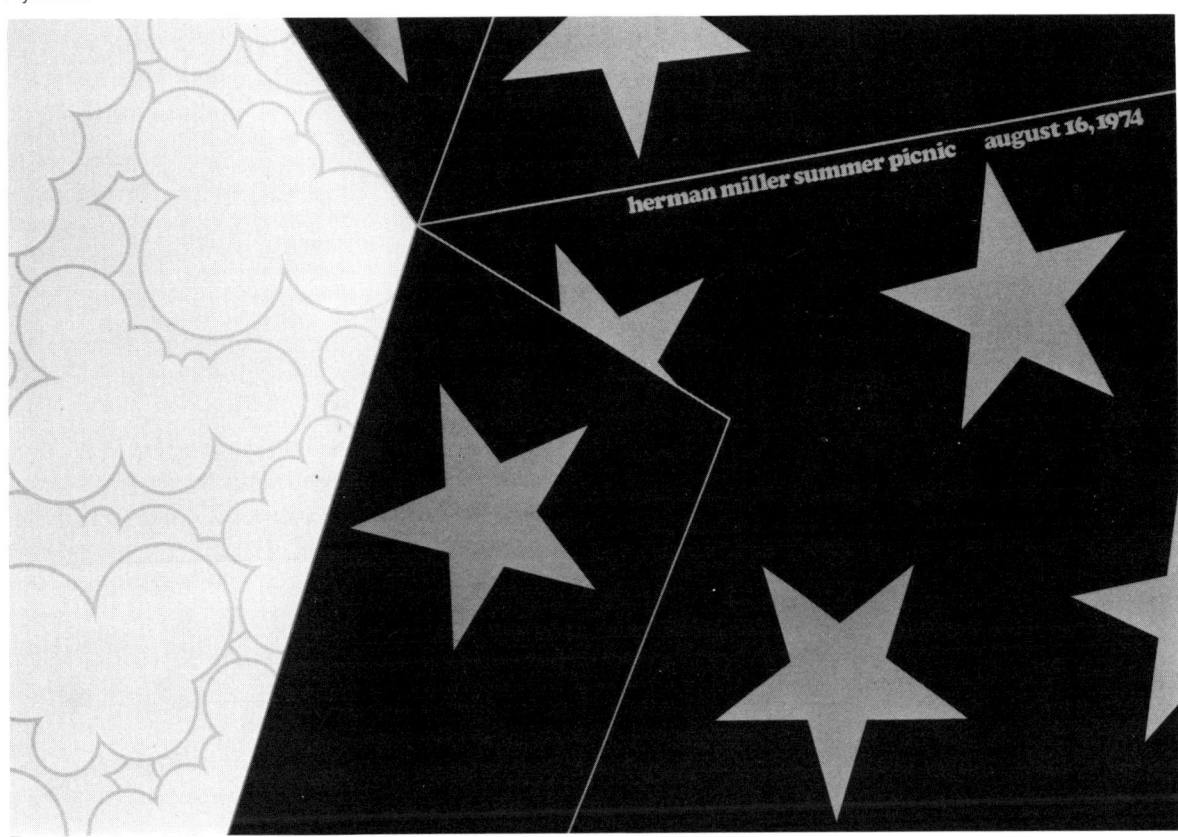

"That all sounds kind of normal when you talk about it," De Pree admits, "because it's the way most companies would do it. But it is not the way we would have done it with Charles. When we introduced the plastic chair, none of us ever asked where we fit into the market or what competitive products were already there. Today there are a lot more of us involved in these decisions, and that confuses people. They get confused if they hear me talking about profits, because they're not used to it. I doubt that D. J. ever talked about profits. And if Vern Poest, the treasurer, talks about good design, *that* confuses people."

"Well," Poest says, "for ten or twelve years I was the only one around here who ever spoke the word *market.*"

"We didn't used to have concepts in this company," says Joe Schwartz. "We used to have philosophies." Those philosophies will remain operational as long as the roots remain alive.

"We're more traditional in our approach, more businesslike," Hugh De Pree says. "But a lot of what D. J. started has carried over into what we're doing today. I think we still have the climate of freedom, the license to rock the boat without being shouted down. Without that I wonder whether we would have accepted Joe Schwartz's initial proposal on how to sell Action Office; or Bob Propst's outfitting an office van for a quadriplegic lawyer.

"And we haven't stopped listening to designers. I never go to see Charles but what we sit down and he racks me over for half a day on what we're doing that we shouldn't be doing. Or he calls and says, 'Is anyone paying any attention to quality around there? Does anyone really care?' "

So Charles scolds. George doesn't even scold any longer. Marketing men are full of enthusiasm. Some of them feel that a burden has been lifted, that their hands have been freed to perform what they identify as the task at hand. But there is a danger. The burden that has been lifted may include the weight, the heft, that has propelled Herman Miller and invested it with excellence for more than fifty years.

The Design of Herman Miller Redesigning the Family Tree

Hugh De Pree (left) and Charles Eames at Milan airport in 1962. "We haven't stopped listening to designers," President De Pree says.

The Design of Herman Miller

New Limbs

A long-time employee observes that "Herman Miller's new wave began when they started moving guys out from New York—Joe Schwartz, Victor Pitzi [vice-president of sales, Office Furniture Group] and Bob Blaich."

Everyone I buttonholed acknowledges, although sometimes grudgingly, that as Herman Miller grows larger the design heritage becomes harder to keep in focus. Robert Blaich is no exception, but he has to do more than just acknowledge the difficulty. As vice-president in charge of design and development, he is responsible for keeping design in focus and for adjusting the focus to the company's new perspectives. Trained as an architect, Blaich joined Herman Miller as a regional sales manager in 1952, during a period when most Herman Miller salesmen had architectural training.

Professionally hyperactive, Blaich lectures at universities and professional gatherings and seems to be present at every design event of consequence in the Western world. (He has been reported to have materialized simultaneously at design conferences oceans apart.)

A Corita poster on Blaich's tackboard proclaims, "He that stays in the valley shall never get over the hill." At first reading that seems reminiscent of Mort Sahl's "The future lies ahead," but it does help explain the direction of the Design and Development Division's current activity.

Blaich's restless labors are related to one of his most important Herman Miller functions: keeping the company in regular communication with the design community. In this respect he acts as a two-way carrier of design information. He explains Herman Miller's policies, products, and services to architects, planners, interior designers, business groups, and students — opening doors that have sometimes been allowed to swing shut in past years. The same activity enables him to know what's going on in the design world, to identify and recruit talent, and to try to see that the fruits of the talent are consistent with Herman Miller objectives.

In 1962, when Blaich began taking over the product development responsibilities that previously had been handled out of George Nelson's office, he saw himself faced with a number of policy options. The first was "to try to do whatever the designers wanted to do, which had been pretty much the design policy for most of Herman Miller's history." Another option was to focus design energies on refining and changing existing products. A third was project development emphasis, such as the O'Hare seating. A fourth option was pure research.

The policy Blaich is trying to pursue includes "a little of each of these, with the chief em-

The Design of Herman Miller New Limbs

Chrome-plated structural steel frameworks designed by Fritz Haller, with a wide variety of interior components.

The Design of Herman Miller New Limbs

Low and high easy chairs and marble table by Poul Kjaerholm.

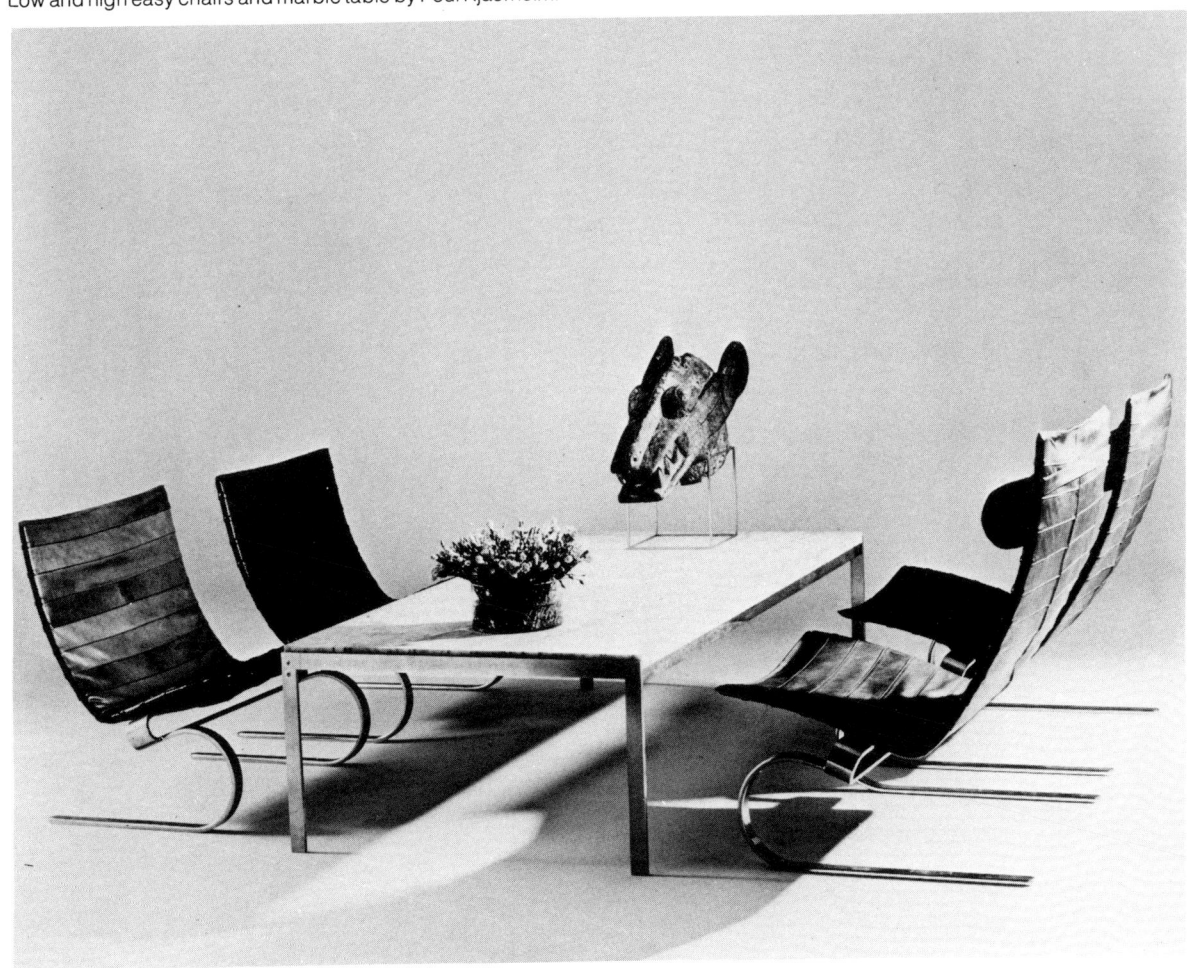

The Design of Herman Miller   New Limbs

Hammock chair with natural cane seat designed by Poul Kjaerholm.

phasis on problem research and problem solving." To this end, he divides his operation into what he calls "effort centers": a design group, a development group, and a facilities group.

The design group consists of consultant designers, independent designers, and internal designers. The development group consists of engineers, developers, and model-makers, and for special projects may be expanded by product development and management specialists from the company at large. The facility-planning staff designs all Herman Miller showrooms, sales offices, and headquarters offices. Its three full-time designers also create exhibitions both in Herman Miller facilities and elsewhere.

Besides directing the Design and Development staff, Blaich acts as liaison with consultants such as Eames and Girard, and with the company's new wave of independent designers, including such established names as Poul Kjaerholm, Fritz Haller, Verner Panton and such newer names as Don Chadwick, Ray Wilkes, Bill Stumpf, and Peter Protzmann. "We can't wrap them up," Blaich says of the independents, "and we don't want to."

Apart from the Design and Development group, Herman Miller has a Systems Design group, headed by Jack Kelley, with its single charter to keep Action Office and Co/Struc moving ahead. It was this group that developed Co/Struc between 1968 and 1973. Another design group, Design Resource Services, headed by Warren Koepf, performs computer analysis of space needs for architects, designers, and end users.

Blaich feels that Herman Miller's new emphases require that Design and Development make a constant attempt to keep products in balance; for example, "great pieces" are to be balanced by systems, middle management work stations are to be balanced by executive suites. In a companywide marketing sense this may be essential. But the company continues also to need something less tidy, something that it has always had. The English poet Roy Fuller once described the lives of certain great writers as characterized by a "fertile lack of balance." Creative instability has its corporate uses too.

During the years that Herman Miller was pioneering modern furniture, the company's graphic design was characterized by a parallel modernity. This was not because of any "corporate identity" program as such. It occurred naturally because graphic material came from the same offices that designed the furniture. But by the midsixties this was no longer true, and John Massey was retained as graphic consultant and charged with establishing a program of corporate consistency.

His first project was a corporate identity manual (retaining the trademark designed by

George Nelson's office, which Massey regarded as uniquely valuable). Then, at Herman Miller's request, he helped set up an Internal Communications Department, responsible for the growing amount of support literature required by the company's newer products. Massey's Chicago office, however, continued to design special corporate publications and the prize-winning annual reports, which are distinguished largely by their radical format, so different in form from other annual reports.

The report one year took the form of an original serigraph, with a perforated and detachable booklet of financial reference. This, Massey felt, was consistent with the company's concern for enriching the working environment. Another year, to emphasize Herman Miller *people,* without resorting to such annual-reportese as shots of grinning plant workers or intensely conferring executives, Massey put together a newsprint composite of the company's own folksy house organs, with an insert containing the information that publicly held companies must provide.

"My objective has always been to give coherence to the company while continuing to relate the graphics to the extreme individuality of the designers reponsible for its reputation," Massey says. "I have never tried to express the philosophy of the company other than in terms of what it makes."

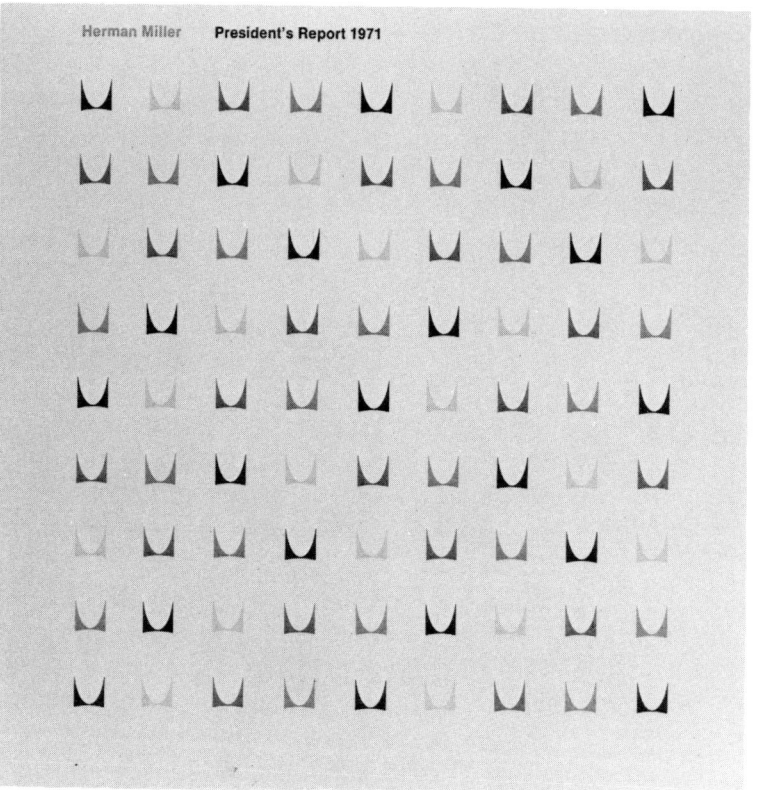

The Design of Herman Miller   New Limbs

108

The Design of Herman Miller   New Limbs

Corporate graphics by John Massey.

Herman Miller
President's Report 1972

Unfortunately, once a company begins to act more like other companies, it begins to talk like other companies. Whether or not Herman Miller's character is threatened by growth and success, its language has begun to suffer already.

The language of Herman Miller past was a charming amalgam of Midwestern idiom filtered through D. J. De Pree's independent perception and subordinated to George Nelson's stunning ability to put the right word in the right place. The literature was always cleanly written, and the house diction studded with such proprietary phrases as *impounded energy* and *providential event*. Eames lent his own craggy descriptive powers to the process—upon first seeing Action Office, he pronounced it "honest ugly."

Herman Miller today is beginning to sound like all the corporations that derive their communicative style from engineering and the social sciences and—worse—from government abuse of language from engineering and the social sciences. Company discourse abounds in *hopefullys* and *thrusts*. The way things are gets less attention than the way things are *positioned* or *perceived*. *Presently* and *at this point in time* mean now; *viable* means feasible, workable, effective, or just all right; *area* and *factor* mean almost anything. *Individual* is used as a noun, *impact* is used as a verb, and *interface, feedback* and *catalyst* are used without any apparent awareness of what these terms mean in the worlds of human factors, cybernetics, and chemistry.

Will it ever improve? Hopefully, with viable feedback. But the individuals I have been interfacing with are not perceived to be repositioning their syntactic thrust in any area at this point in time.

The Design of Herman Miller Shoptalk

"Word processing" is a centralized operation using dictating machines and high-speed electric typewriters with magnetic control units to produce typewritten material. Action Office components and accessories are used in Word Processing Centers.

To some, Herman Miller is indistinguishable from D. J. De Pree and—by extension—from Zeeland, Michigan. However, De Pree is far from a typical hometown product. In a town dominated by Republicans and the Reformed theology, he is a Democrat and a Baptist. He was actually in Democratic politics before he was old enough to vote: when Governor-elect Woodbridge Ferris, a Democrat, drove through Zeeland in a victory parade, the teenaged De Pree rode with him, because the town didn't have enough adult Democrats to fill the car.

D. J., like most people born in Zeeland near the turn of the century, was baptized in the Reformed Church. He began veering away from it in the early thirties. "For one thing, they believed in infant baptism, and I couldn't find any reference to that in the Bible, which told me that people became Christians not as infants but by being born again." Another quarrel with Reformed doctrine included his "acceptance of the Biblical view of Israel as an unconsumable nation."

In the early thirties, D. J. met a man who had talked the Park Township Board of Education into letting him use a run-down schoolhouse for evening religious meetings. D. J. helped him set up regular nondenominational meetings on Thursday evenings, and these were so popular they began holding them on Sundays as well. In the midfifities, the town built a new school, and the informal congregation bought the old school building as the basis for a new Baptist church, which was completed in the early sixties. As recently as 1973, De Pree gave a speech to the Zeeland Chamber of Commerce, arguing that the Reformed theological monopoly in town had to be broken.

"There is, of course, much more to D. J. than just being a Christian," says Max De Pree, "but Christian activities have occupied most of his nonbusiness life. He was active in various kinds of missionary activities, including the Gideon Society, which he headed internationally for three years."

"I never had any hobbies," D. J. says. "No golf . . . I never joined Rotary. I felt that what I was doing was a lot more important and that I couldn't take time from either family or business for hobbies. My religious work made for a change of pace in my way of thinking on Thursday and Friday evenings and all day on Sunday."

Apart from the change of pace for D. J., how important is religion in the company? Many employees in Zeeland describe the company as Christian. However, Max De Pree says: "Although religious conviction is a key part of the process that has brought us where we are, Herman Miller is not a Christian company, and it would be a serious mistake to call it that." Charles Eames affirms this: "The makeup of the company is not religious. You know, it was really George who introduced

D. J. to honest-to-God Christian working principles."

In any case the long-lasting love affair between D. J. and George was enhanced by their religious differences, which lent humor and bite to the relationship. Non-Christians have played an extremely important role in the development of Herman Miller. Charles Eames, who is at least psychologically Jewish, describes Jimmy Eppinger as "having qualities strongly flavored by a chicken soup attitude toward all human ills. He had a good deal of Jewish body English of a kind not seen in Zeeland at the time he appeared."

"As a matter of fact," D. J. recalls, "I think Jimmy Eppinger became more Jewish as I talked to him."

"We took a kind of chicken soup approach to Action Office 1," Milly Teperman, the licensee for Brazil, acknowledges. "We knew it was being sold in the states as a systems concept, but we sold the desks simply as desks, and architects were charmed by them. It wasn't what Propst had in mind, I knew, but at that time, in Brazil, we needed chicken soup."

The late Bishop Pike used to resent the characterization of religion as a narrow concept, when one of the things that attracted *him* to it was its roominess, the varieties of experience it could contain and address. The roominess of D. J.'s thinking has affected the company he founded more than any specific theological content has.

"I never saw anything *un*-Christian about business," D. J. says. "The Bible says you can't *serve* God and mammon, but that's just a question of who's boss. I really believe that everything here happened because of what God did, not because we were worthy."

Thumb through any corporation's annual report, promotional brochures, or house organs and the odds are that you'll come to a line that reads something like this: "The Ajax Valve Company Is People."

It's true, of course—as how could it not be?—of Ajax and every other company, including Herman Miller. And it follows that the differences between companies are differences between people. But since it has been authoritatively reported that people are pretty much the same the world over, how are the differences established and sustained? It is reasonable to suppose that it has something to do with a company attitude toward people—the way they are recruited, rewarded, and, above all, regarded. Inevitably, then, it begins with management.

When I began researching this book, I looked for an organizational chart, but couldn't find one. There is no official table of organization. (There are, however, dozens of unofficial ones.)

"There has always been a certain resistance to that kind of thing around here," I was told. "If you believe people are equal under God, you don't put them above and below each other."

But they *are* above and below each other within the company. People at Herman Miller have bosses, even though they call them, and everyone else in the company, by their first names. Corporate hierarchy is acknowledged here as anywhere else in industry, through responsibilities, titles, salaries, even (despite the egalitarian implication of open-plan Action Office work stations) private offices. It is not status that the company resists, but *publication* of status, in an almost superstitious nod to human equality.

The assumption of equal worth, coupled with the recognition of not-necessarily-equal contributions, makes it possible for a complementary mix of people to have a synergetic force. This is not to say that Herman Miller is all one family or that if it were it would be an incessantly happy one. Behind the camaraderie of picnics and parties (made memorable with posters by graphic design director Steve Frykholm) are all the concerns of any real world: backbiting, slights both real and imagined, perceived injustices.

"Herman Miller is an extremely political company," a salesman remarks, "but everyone acts as though the politics don't exist."

After outlining corporate philosophy and objectives, Hugh De Pree adds that these "come to life through the action and performance of people." One element of conscious control for bringing them to life is the Scanlon Plan of joint incentive.

This too is a matter of roots. The Scanlon Plan at Herman Miller owes as much to D. J. as does the molded plywood chair and for the same reason: his openness to someone else's idea.

"Back when we were facing bankruptcy," De Pree recalls, "the Lord began to deal with me on the way I was treating employees. Oh, I knew everyone's name. When you have 80 employees, that's not too hard. But I didn't really know *them*."

This was brought home pointedly after the plant's millwright dropped dead on the shipping room floor. Visiting the family, D. J. discovered that the man had written poetry and made things. For the first time it occurred to him that he was in effect riding herd on a group of men and women whose worth as individuals, apart from their work, he had not considered. And if he hadn't considered it, how could he arrange to tap their creative potential?

Consideration wasn't enough. Workers were at the mercy of management's impotent and frenzied guessing. If there were no sales, there was no work. "I was in no position to do right by them," D. J. points out, "and there was no union to make me behave."

In 1950, D. J. and Hugh De Pree went to a meeting of the Grand Rapids Furniture Manufacturers Association to hear a Michigan State University professor named Carl Frost speak on cost accounting. Frost, however, didn't talk about accounting; he talked about something called the Scanlon Plan, and during the drive back to Zeeland, the De Prees decided to look into the matter.

Soon afterward, D. J. called on Frost in Lansing and found him teaching in a Quonset hut. "He was reticent," D. J. remembers, "feeling us out I think, trying to decide whether we really meant what we said. But he came to Zeeland to talk with people in the plant, and on that occasion he used profanity. I thought it was just window dressing, and I still do. He looked like a Lutheran minister."

Frost agreed to set up a Scanlon Plan at Herman Miller, with the stipulation that the De Prees themselves participate and share in the bonuses. The Scanlon concept of equity calls for an investment on the part of everyone in the company, a recognition that individual incentives differ greatly, and an insistence that each participant get a fair return on his investment. As a start the company put 30 cents from every dollar of sales into the payroll, including all management salaries.

The plant was operating on a piecework basis then and Frost stopped all piecework at once, because he thought it competitive in the wrong way. A good worker was not eager to share his effective techniques with others. "You have one common competitor," Frost told them, "other furniture manufacturers."

Named for labor-management strategist Joseph Scanlon, the Scanlon Plan is not a simple incentive scheme. It is a fairly complex means of organizing an entire company to increase productivity and share the benefits of the increase. Scanlon is particularly well suited to Herman Miller because it operates from Douglas McGregor's "Theory Y" premise — that work is a natural activity and that people require responsibility and will welcome it in a climate of organized incentive.

Scanlon is based on participation and equity. All Zeeland employees are represented in a network of production and screening committees, and all share in bonuses based upon the resultant productivity. The plan's implementation depends upon constant communication of what is going on in the company each day, and this communication is one of the prime responsibilities of Richard Ruch, vice-president in charge of manufacturing.

The manufacture of Action Office equipment thrived under the plan, growing from a 2 million per month volume to a 4 million per month volume in 5 years. But Scanlon incorporates quality into productivity as well. There are no roving inspectors in Action Office assembly operations. Each workman is his own inspector, and the next person to see the product after assembly is the customer.

Terry Vande Water, editor of in-house publications, believes one reason the plan works so well at Herman Miller is that Zeeland people are quality oriented to begin with. Some see Scanlon as yet another case of a Providential Happening that became incorporated into the company's way of life, a logical extension of the growth pattern D. J. De Pree started in the thirties. D. J. himself sees it as "a tool, a great way to implement the idea that *everyone* in business has a right to identity, equity, and opportunity. The children of employees should be able to say, 'This is my Dad's factory.' Employees should be paid on a basis that is equitable not only within the company but within the community and the industry. And there ought to be stairways of promotion that are easy to locate."

Scanlon is not a panacea and so far it has failed to reverse economic laws. Herman Miller is subject to the same troubles that beset other corporations in time of recession, and there have been layoffs. But the plan's emphasis on companywide productivity has tended at least to minimize layoffs caused by increased efficiency alone. "A few years ago we cut Action Office labor and materials cost 10 percent without hurting a guy on the floor," Ruch says.

Is Scanlon a mechanism for circumventing a union? Answers are various: "Herman Miller employees would never stand for a union." "Historically, there have never been unions in Zeeland." "Scanlon is actually the equivalent of a union." "Scanlon is far superior to any union in benefits." D. J. De Pree says simply: "I think we can get along without a union, but I think they are absolutely necessary in some places. One of the greatest things Roosevelt ever did was to open the door."

When Frost came in (at a $75 per day consulting fee paid not to him but to Michigan State University), the plant was nearly out of control. Deliveries were as much as 26 weeks late; resources, including management resources, were being squandered. All three De Prees were personally involved at times with inspecting items as they left the plant. They were capable of doing it — D. J. because of his years of observation, Max and Hugh because they had actually worked in a variety of factory jobs (they are both master upholsterers). Nevertheless, Frost told them that was not their job and got them to turn that responsibility over to others.

"He taught me that the problems are at the top," D. J. says. Frost taught them too that paternalism was no way to serve the employees or anyone else. "In the old days," a salesman remarks, "they never fired anyone. They just didn't know how, couldn't bring themselves to do it." But Frost told D. J., "You are not Santa Claus. Everyone has to cut the mustard."

"Everyone," of course, included Hugh and Max as well, a fact that took on special importance in 1970 when Herman Miller went public. "Then we really had to become professional managers," Max De Pree says.

Frost challenged the De Prees' outside activities as well, if they took time and energy away from Herman Miller. In 1951, when D. J. was elected president of Gideon International, Frost urged him to consider the consequences for Herman Miller. (He did, but took on the presidency.) When Hugh De Pree assumed the heavy responsibilities of chairman of the Hope College board of trustees, Frost questioned the diversion of time, energy and concentration from Herman Miller. (At this writing, Hugh remains chairman of the board.)

Frost still looks like a Lutheran minister, with a surface blandness that belies the extremely important, if not always visible, role he has in the corporation. People at all levels of the company consult him on matters at all levels of complexity. Recently, he has advised management about personnel changes, counseled plant workers about domestic problems, helped circumvent a departmental rift, and influenced the design of a birthday gift for an overseas licensee.

While his own corporate role defies definition, Frost has been sharply instrumental in defining the roles of others, and the process of continual definition may be the key to his contribution. His own modest job description seems to square with this view. As a clinical psychologist in a mental hospital, Frost used to ask patients, "What day is it?" The answer was one indication of the patient's connection with reality. "That's really my role at Herman Miller," he says. "I keep asking them, 'What day is it?'"

The Design of Herman Miller Collision Insurance

The Herman Miller story is made up of many Herman Miller stories, some of them contradictory and many of them corny. Not to worry. Clichés hold truths, and they too are contradictory. "The best things in life are free" — at least to people who can afford them. "Absence makes the heart grow fonder" is precisely as valid as "out of sight, out of mind." When people at Herman Miller started talking to me about "a company with a heart," I used to wince. I still wince, but by now it is mostly just a nervous reflex.

As chancellor of the University of Chicago, Robert Hutchins was often asked how he had managed to make the university so good. He had a stock reply: "It's not really a very good university. But it's the best one there is." Herman Miller Inc. may not be as good a company as its warmest supporters say it is, but it is a remarkable company, and the ways in which it is remarkable account for its astonishing influence in modern design.

Are companies really different from each other? "Well," a Herman Miller executive replies, "they are not as different as people, but they are as different as families."

It is a useful analogy. Like other kinds of families, Herman Miller is experiencing generational differences, forced examination of values in a changing society, and other pressures. As with families, the more severe the pressure of the present, the simpler the past looks.

"As we get bigger and bigger," a vice-president observes, "certain values become hard to hold on to or even keep in sight." There are few companies that are as aware of the problem as Herman Miller is, and few companies as aware that the solution is not necessarily at hand.

"Herman Miller never became what Charles wanted it to become or what George wanted it to become," Max De Pree says. "For that matter, it has not become what D. J. wanted it to become either."

George Nelson told me, "At Herman Miller each phase of development gave you freedom to do more things; the new tools led to new expectations and satisfied them. But long ago it was clear that the company was destined to run head-on into Steelcase."

In curiously similar language, Max told me, "It can't be the kind of company it has been for years. I see a kind of collision course between quality as D. J. understood it and some of the things we are doing now."

The best collision insurance is a clear sense of where you are going, and perhaps the best way for a corporation to sense that is to know where the corporate vitality comes from. Roots again. The initial uniqueness of Her-

The Design of Herman Miller Collision Insurance

man Miller Inc. lay in D. J. De Pree's ability to get strength from other people and to arrange for that strength to be deposited in designed products as impounded energy.

"Herman Miller has always operated with the designer as the creative force," Hugh De Pree says. Perhaps the most important consequence of that force has been the design of Herman Miller itself.